What Is Man?

What Is Man?

formerly: Man: Ruined and Restored

Leslie B. Flynn

This book is designed for your personal reading pleasure and profit. It is also designed for group study. A leader's guide with helps and hints for teachers is available from your local Christian bookstore or from the publisher.

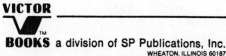

VICTOR ™
BOOKS a division of SP Publications, Inc.
WHEATON, ILLINOIS 60187

Offices also in
Whitby, Ontario, Canada
Amersham-on-the-Hill, Bucks, England

About the Author

Leslie B. Flynn is pastor of Grace Conservative Baptist Church, Nanuet, New York. He is a graduate of Moody Bible Institute, Wheaton College, Eastern Baptist Theological Seminary (B.D.), and the University of Pennsylvania (M.A.). He received an honorary doctorate from Conservative Baptist Theological Seminary in 1963. He is author of other Victor Books titles: *19 Gifts of the Spirit, Dare to Care Like Jesus, The Gift of Joy, God's Will: You Can Know It* (written with his wife, Bernice), *Joseph: God's Man in Egypt,* and *The Twelve.*

Other books in the "Basic Doctrine Series":

Who Is Jesus? by Bruce A. Demarest
What Is the Church? by Bruce L. Shelley
Is the Bible Reliable? by Robert L. Saucy

Unless otherwise noted, all Scripture quotations are taken from the *King James Version.* Another version used is *The Old Testament: Confraternity Version* (CON), © 1965 by Guild Press, New York, New York.

Library of Congress Catalog Card Number: 82-61572
ISBN: 0-88207-104-1

VICTOR BOOKS
a division of SP Publications, Inc.
P.O. Box 1825 • Wheaton, Illinois 60187

Contents

1

What Is Man?

What is man? We ask this question in the maternity ward when a baby's cry signals a new life. We ask it in the death chamber when a soul feebly departs its body, leaving behind loved ones. We stand on a street corner and, as we watch the crowds hurry by to work, we wonder, why work? To eat. Why eat? To have strength to work.

We rise in the morning, dash to the office, return home for dinner and a little relaxation, then go to bed. Next morning we repeat the same round of activity.

A backwoods woman at a county fair was angry with her husband, who somehow had managed to get hold of a quarter to ride on the merry-go-round. A miser in her handling of the family purse strings, she felt this to be a foolish waste of money. When the merry-go-round came to a stop, she was waiting for him. "What's the big idea?" she asked. "You got off where you got on! You spent a whole quarter, and you ain't been nowhere!"

Many would echo her words. The years have slipped by, we've spent money, time, and energy, and what have we accomplished?

People ask many questions:

What is life all about?

What was man like at the beginning?

Can we believe the story of Adam and Eve eating the forbidden fruit?

Why should Adam's sin be imputed to following generations?

Is man more than body? If so, is he two parts, body and soul, or three parts, body, soul, and spirit?

Where does his soul come from? God or his parents?

Is there life after death?

Will there be a resurrection of the body?

Man Is a Paradox

Man is not only a puzzle, but he's also a paradox. His ingenuity builds jets that fly 600 miles per hour, but worldwide airport security is required lest those products of his genius be hijacked or blown to pieces.

A New York City policeman said, "We send a man to the moon but we can't even make him go to the back of the bus."

Man can wallow in the gutter, yet he is able to compose music. French philosopher and scientific genius, Blaise Pascal, once observed both the degradation and the dignity of man. "What a chimera then is man! What a monster, what a chaos, what a contradiction, what a prodigy! Judge of all things; imbecile worm of the earth; depository of truth; a sink of uncertainty and error; the pride and refuse of the universe." At one moment man is a Dr. Jekyll; at the next a Mr. Hyde.

Because of this paradox of man—on the one hand, evil; on the other hand, noble—we have two sharply contrasting but erroneous views of man, which may be simply termed the low view and the high view.

The low view conceives of man made wholly of material substance; even his capacity to think is seen as nothing but the activity of his bodily, chemical processes. One modern example of this view is B. F. Skinner's behaviorism, which regards man as only another animal. He is considered more complex than other animals and more difficult to control, yet he is nevertheless as controllable as every other animal through the manipulation of his environment.

The contrasting high view of man holds that man has a divine spark, which only needs fanning into a flame of goodness, enabling him to master his own nature and effect his own salvation. This concept leads to virtual self-deification.

The Christian view of man takes into consideration both his animallike behavior and his divine potential. The Psalmist David, as a lonely shepherd on a night vigil, meditated on the radiant moon and the sparkling stars, and counted man unworthy of God's attention. Yet he remembered that the Lord watches over the least of men. "When I consider Thy heavens, the work of Thy fingers, the moon and the stars, which Thou hast ordained; What is man that Thou art mindful of him?" (Ps. 8:3-4)

Lost in the vastness of the universe, man is nothing. But as the object of God's care, man is everything. Man is a combination of pygmy and giant. He is puny but powerful, insignificant and important. He is ignoble yet noble, mortal and immortal.

Man and the Universe

A scientist once suggested an interesting analogy. Imagine, he said, a perfectly smooth glass pavement on which the finest speck can be seen. Then shrink our sun from 865,000 miles in diameter to only 2 feet, and place this gilt ball on the pavement to represent the sun.

Step off 82 paces of about 2 feet each, and to proportionately represent the first planet, Mercury, put down a mustard seed.

Take 60 steps more, each about 2 feet, and for Venus, put down an ordinary shot the size of a beebee.

Mark 78 steps more, and for our earth, put down a pea.

Step off 108 paces from there, and for Mars, put down a pinhead.

Sprinkle some fine dust for the asteroids, take 788 steps more, and for Jupiter, put down an orange.

Take 934 steps, and for Saturn, put down a golf ball.

Mark 2,086 steps more, and for Uranus, put down a marble.

Step off 2,322 steps from there, and for Neptune, put down a cherry.

This will take 2½ miles, and we haven't discussed Pluto. If we swing completely around, we have a smooth glass surface 5 miles in diameter, representing our solar system, just a tiny fraction of the heavens. On this surface, 5 miles across, we have only a mustard seed, beebee, pea, pinhead, dust, orange, golf ball, a marble, and a cherry. And we should have to go 6,720 miles, not feet, on the same scale before we could put down another 2-foot ball to represent the nearest star.

A first-floor room in New York City's Hayden Planetarium contains a miniature replica of our solar system, showing comparative speeds and sizes of our planets. But this replica doesn't depict the three outer planets, Uranus, Neptune, and Pluto. Uranus would be in the planetarium's outer corridor, Neptune outside near Eighth Avenue, and Pluto would be three long avenues away on Fifth. On the same scale the nearest star would be in Cleveland, Ohio!

Astronauts tell us how on their journey moonward the earth became a little blue ball. Physically man may be six feet tall and weigh 200 pounds, but he is only an infinitesimal fraction of the earth's size. And if the earth be a little ball, then how small is man!

A friend of Teddy Roosevelt told how he and Roosevelt used to play a little game when they were visiting each other. After an evening of conversation they would go outside on a clear night and search the skies until one or the other found a faint speck of light-mist in a certain spot in the sky. Then he would recite,

That is the Spiral Galaxy in Andromeda.
That speck is as large as our Milky Way.
It is one of a hundred million galaxies.
It consists of one hundred billion suns,
each larger than our sun.

Then he would conclude, "Now that we have our perspective, let's go to bed!"

Man and the Elements

Not only in relation to the vast universe, but also in comparison to the power of the earth's elements, man is almost as nothing. If the earth quakes, if the wind whirls into a tornado, if clouds withhold rain, man is utterly helpless.

Man and Atomic Discoveries

If you saw a traveler at Kennedy Airport call five redcaps to help move an object the size of a matchbox, you would be amused. If the object were opened and found empty except for one little speck of matter, you would be dumbfounded. And if the speck were put on scales and shown to weigh several tons, you would rub your eyes in amazement. Yet scientists affirm that a speck could weigh several tons, if its empty spaces were eliminated and its constituent parts packed together.

Empty spaces in matter, you say? Yes, we know that matter is not a hard substance filling space, but an empty void in which tiny particles, protons, and electrons revolve at speeds so fast we cannot photograph them. Matter is composed of molecules which in turn are composed of atoms with their swirling protons and electrons. These atoms are so small that 5,000 of them could be placed in a row on the period at the end of this sentence.

Remember how vast a space there is between the stars? Yet proportionately there is more space between atoms than between stars. If all the empty spaces in a 220-pound football fullback could be eliminated, he could be compressed to the size of a speck of dust invisible to the naked eye—which isn't a very flattering thought.

Man's Brevity

Someone said that man's history can be summed up in terms of three tablets: school tablet, aspirin tablet, and stone tablet.

Man lives such a short span contrasted with the centuries of history. Months are spent in infancy, in sleeping, eating, sickness, and frailty, with not much time left over for serious work. No wonder the Bible speaks of life as a tale that is told, a flower that fades, grass that withers, a shadow that declines, smoke that evaporates, and vapor that vanishes (Ps. 90:9, 5-6; Job 14:2; Ps. 102:11; 103:15; James 4:14).

Someone described the passing of the years as the teachable teens, tender twenties, tireless thirties, fiery forties, forceful fifties, serious sixties, sacred seventies, aching eighties, shortening breath, death, the sod, God.

It doesn't take long to move from the layette to the layout.

Man's Inhumanity to Man

Man builds up cities, bombs them to bits, then proceeds to rebuild them out of the rubble. Man makes undreamed-of scientific advances, then makes a science out of destroying life.

Within every person is a built-in defect, a bent to do evil. Why is it that when a rival falls, our first impulse is glee? Why all the feuding, rioting, and violence? When a Copenhagen TV station showed a film on bullfighting, complaints forced them to take it off. What did they substitute? A naval battle!

Historians tell us that when Galileo showed the senators of Florence, Italy his new telescope, their immediate reaction was, "That glass will be a great advantage to us in time of war!" Today our world stands poised on the brink of a hydrogen hell that could wipe out vast portions of the population. In this respect man hasn't changed much.

Man's Importance

Though insignificant, man is in a special sense important. After David noted how puny man was in contrast to the star-studded sky, he added, "Thou, O Lord, art mindful of him." The point of this eighth psalm is that the God who made the heavens condescends to care for man, to be interested in him, even to visit earth.

Man's Creation

Just as people get their heads together to plan, so the triune God conferred before the creation of man, agreeing, "Let us make man" (Gen. 1:26). Thus, man is the outcome of divine planning.

Not only did God decide to make man, but the divine Trinity made man in the image and likeness of God. Trees don't resemble God, and animals are not created in God's image. But man, with special mental and moral capacities, is unique in God's creation. Our sense of insignificance dwindles when we realize this.

The image of God in man—which we will explore in a later

chapter—gives a sense of dignity and certain rights of freedom to man. This is why the American Founding Fathers in the Declaration of Independence spoke of self-evident truths, namely that "all men are created equal; that they are endowed by their Creator with certain unalienable rights; that among these are life, liberty and the pursuit of happiness." Man has these rights because he is made in the divine image.

On the other hand, totalitarianism believes that man was made for the state; as Mussolini, typical of all Fascist and Communist dictators, said, "All individuals are relative, only to be conceived of in their relations to the State." In such thinking, ordinary men are raw material for manipulation by men who consider themselves superior. Marxists consider man important only as he may be used to establish a classless society. But Christianity teaches that all men are equal in God's sight, created in His image, and an individual's interests are not to be subordinate to or smothered by operations of the state. Because of his inherent dignity and worth, man should be esteemed, not exploited.

Man Is at the Apex of Creation

Man is superior to animate and inanimate nature. Unlike the animals, he can reason, speak, appreciate beauty, invent, exercise moral choice, and worship. Though man's feet walk on the earth, his mind reaches heavenward.

Animals have no zoos to display captured humans, but people design cages to show off animals. Who runs the circus: animals or humans? You may see artists sketching at the zoo, but you have never seen a giraffe painting a person.

Who gets a license to hunt for prey—man or animal? Unless hungry or wounded, beasts usually don't attack men. The Psalmist tells why, "Thou madest him to have dominion over the works of Thy hands; Thou has put all things under his feet: All sheep and oxen, yea, and the beasts of the field; the fowl of the air, and the fish of the sea, and whatsoever passeth through the paths of the seas" (8:6-8).

Even the vast Milky Way is inferior to a human being. A skeptic, trying to belittle man in our vast astronomical universe, argued, "What is man in comparison with all these galaxies?" A believer quietly replied, "Man is the astronomer." Yes, men study the stars; the stars never study man.

Pascal said that man is but a reed, the most feeble thing in nature, able to be snapped by the weight of a feathery sparrow, but he is a thinking reed. He added, "If the universe were to crush man, man would still be more noble than that which killed him, because he knows that he dies, and he knows the advantage which the universe holds over him. But the universe knows nothing of this."

In the fifth century Augustine, Bishop of Hippo, wrote these words, which were inscribed 15 centuries later in the Hall of Fame at New York's World of Tomorrow:

> Man wonders over the restless sea,
> The flowing water, the sight of the sky,
> And forgets that of all wonders
> Man himself is the most wonderful.

God Became Man

God actually linked Himself with man in what is termed the Incarnation. God became Man in the person of Jesus Christ. The One who upholds all things by the word of His power, came down to earth to become one of us. As the Bible puts it, "In the beginning was the Word . . . All things were made by Him . . . And the Word was made flesh, and dwelt among us" (John 1:1, 3, 14).

A thousand years after David, watching the stars from Bethlehem fields, asked the question, "What is man?" shepherds under the same stars saw the heavens open for angels to announce the birth of the Saviour. In answer to David's question, the importance of man was shown by God's coming to earth to link Himself to mankind.

Because Adam dragged the race down through disobedience, the second Adam, Jesus Christ, came to lift us up through perfect obedience. He stooped that we might be raised. He took on human nature that we might share His divine nature. The writer of Hebrews stated, "For verily He took not on Him the nature of angels; but He took on Him the seed of Abraham" (2:16).

He didn't masquerade as a man, but as the Nicene Creed put it, He "was incarnated by the Holy Ghost of the Virgin Mary; and was made man." No other creature in all the universe can claim that he bears the flesh worn by Deity.

The Athanasian Creed of the fourth century speaks of the Incarnation as "not the conversion of the Godhead into flesh, but [the] taking [of] the manhood into God." Thomas Howard calls this "the mystery of our flesh raised to glory" ("God Before Birth: The Imagery Matters," in *Christianity Today,* Dec. 17, 1976, p. 11).

All who are linked to the God-man Redeemer shall someday be like Him. In the meantime, redeemed human beings, who have partaken of the divine nature, are useful instruments in God's hands. They are on earth for a purpose, men and women of destiny.

Some years ago, a group of Abyssinians had an argument with a visiting Englishman. As a result, the Englishman was jailed without trial, then later removed to the dungeon of Magdala deep in Abyssinian territory. Six months went by before the British government learned of the incident and demanded his immediate release. The demand was haughtily rejected by Abyssinian King Theodore. When a second demand was refused, the British decided to act.

Within a few days ships loaded with arms and soldiers left England. Weeks later the armada reached Abyssinia. British soldiers fought their way easily to the walls of Magdala. Storming the dungeon, they released the unjustly treated Englishman. Jubilantly they headed back to their ship, then to England. When the cost of the expedition was figured up, it was discovered that the rescue of one Englishman from that Abyssinian dungeon cost the British government the equivalent of $25 million.

This sum, though staggering, was nothing compared with the cost to God to rescue lost men. To redeem fallen humans "God so loved the world that He gave His only begotten Son" (John 3:16).

How fitting that Apollo astronauts should have deposited in a sealed capsule on the moon's surface these words from Psalm 8:

When [we] behold [the] heavens, the work of
Your fingers, the moon and the stars which
You set in place—
What is man that You should be mindful
of him, or the son of man that You should
care for him? (vv. 3-4, CON)

2

Where Did Man Come From?

A little boy, visiting the blacksmith's shop at the Williamsburg Restoration Village in Virginia, turned to his father and said, "Daddy, now I know where horses come from."

"Where?" asked his father.

"From the blacksmith. He makes them."

"Where did you get that idea?" pursued his father.

"See," said the boy, "he's finishing a horse now. He's nailing on his shoes!"

We smile at his naive judgment. Yet modern science, examining the available data of nature, has theorized that our universe evolved from a piece of primordial ooze. It supposes that through some inherent force everything that exists has developed in an unbroken line all the way from molecule to man.

Despite the fact that the evolutionary interpretation is still only an assumption, it is the accepted explanation for man's origin throughout the secular educational system. Attempts have been made recently, notably in California and Texas, to require the creationist view of the origin of life to be presented alongside the evolutionary hypothesis in public school science courses. Creationists hold that a true explanation of the facts of nature requires the intervention of a divine Creator.

In a monograph published by the American Scientific Affiliation, Dr. Russell L. Mixter, for many years Professor of Zoology at Wheaton College, stresses the problem of gaps between major groups of organisms. He summarizes thus: "The earliest representatives of the major groups of animals and plants are complex organisms. They are separated by structural gaps from the members of other groups. As long as the gaps remain unbridged by a series of fossils grading between one group and another, one may conclude that the ancestors of the groups are created and not descended from other orders."

Mixter readily admits that within the orders and families, descent with modification does exist, as in the series of horses. However, until fossil evidence indicates that "a major group of organisms, such as an order, is connected to another order by a closely graded series of forms, one need not hold the [evolutionary] interpretation which derives the members of one order from some other order" (*Creation and Evolution,* American Scientific Affiliation, 1950, p. 23).

The gap between man and the highest animal is so great that man's existence can only be explained by divine creative fiat.

The Biblical Account

The scriptural record is found in the first chapter of Genesis: "So God created man in His own image, in the image of God created He him; male and female created He them" (1:27).

Because another narrative appears in the second chapter, critics claim a contradiction between the episodes, or conclude that another writer's version has been woven into the record by an editor. In reality, the accounts are not contradictory, but complementary. The first chapter places man as the last and highest of God's creation. The second chapter is a restatement of the first, plus additional facts, describing man's creation in greater detail than that of other created things.

According to the expanded record, Adam was created first. "And the Lord God formed man of the dust of the ground, and breathed into his nostrils the breath of life; and man became a living soul" (Gen. 2:7).

Then we have Eve's creation. "And the Lord God caused a deep sleep to fall upon Adam, and he slept; and He took one of his ribs, and closed up the flesh instead thereof. And the rib, which the Lord God had taken from man, made He a woman, and brought her unto the man" (2:21-22).

Formed from Dust

A little girl excitedly asked her mother, "Is it true that we are made from dust, and when we die we go back to dust?"

Mother replied, "Yes, it's true."

The little girl exclaimed, "I just looked under my bed. And there's someone either coming or going!"

When it came time for man to appear, God took dust (elements which He had previously created) and formed man's body. Approximately 20 of the one hundred or so known elements are found in the human body. "The Lord God formed man of the dust of the ground."

Because the bodies of animals were also formed out of the ground (Gen. 2:19), a common relation exists between man and animal. Man is sometimes defined as a "thinking animal." But it does not follow that man evolved from the brute. What we can affirm is that the bodies of both animal and man were formed of the same elemental substance, and by a common Creator.

Some believe that God used the fully developed body of some previous animal form to make man. Dr. Carl F. H. Henry, noted theologian, says, "The narrative does not rule out the possibility of God's use and transformation of a prior animal form; but it does not specifically assert this, nor can it be held actually to imply it. No such 'implication' was found in the passage by exegetes until after the rise of the evolutionary theory" (*Christianity Today,* May 21, 1965, p. 16).

Among other elements, someone estimated that the human body contains:

> enough sulphur to rid a dog of fleas
> enough lime to whitewash a chicken coop
> enough fat for six bars of soap
> enough iron for a few dozen nails

> enough phosphorus for 20 boxes of matches
> enough magnesium for a dose of magnesia
> enough sugar for 10 cups of coffee
> enough potassium to explode a toy cannon
> enough salt for 20 spoonfuls

When man is viewed as no more than a body, the logical outcome is to treat people as animals. But man is worth far more than the total value of his bodily elements. Man is a unique combination of the dust of the earth and the breath of God.

A Living Soul

It is not surprising that man's body originated from the earth, when we recall that man must continually ingest the minerals of the earth to sustain his existence, and that at death man again becomes part of the earth.

Man's body was formed from the dust of the earth, fashioned by God, then through a special spiration of God, was made a living soul. God "breathed into his nostrils the breath of life; and man became a living soul" (Gen. 2:7).

Living soul in the Genesis account refers not so much to a distinct aspect of man's being but denotes his body animated with the life of God. We know this because animals, too, are said to derive their life from God's spirit (Ps. 104:30); and the term "living creature," used for animals in Genesis 1:24, is the same Hebrew expression translated "living soul" when referring to Adam in Genesis 2:7.

What then distinguishes man from animals, if both are living creatures or living souls? It is this—when God breathed into man's nostrils the breath of life, He created a part of man in His own divine image. "In the image of God created He him" (Gen. 1:27). Man possessed both a material part and an immaterial part. God formed his physical element out of preexisting materials, but He formed his metaphysical element *ex nihilo,* out of that which did not previously exist, creating it in the image of Himself. This is what makes man of measureless worth. (A fuller explanation of the meaning of the image of God will be found in the following chapter.)

The total value of the material part of man is only a few dollars; it is the immaterial part of man that makes him priceless. Physically, man is but a parasite on the skin of a tiny planet, related to polywogs and pigs, and somewhat resembling apes and monkeys. Metaphysically, according to Jesus, man is of greater value than flowers, birds, sheep, even the entire world. Didn't He ask, "For what is man profited, if he shall gain the whole world, and lose his own soul? or what shall a man give in exchange for his soul?" (Matt. 16:26; see also 6:26, 30; 12:12)

As Dr. Vernon Grounds, president of Conservative Baptist Theological Seminary, puts it, "How difficult to believe that a lust-crazed drunkard on Skid Row in Chicago or on the Bowery in New York is worth more than all the diamonds that have ever been dug out of South African mines . . . that a naked cannibal on a Pacific Island is worth more than all the money in our American banks . . . that an Oriental beggar, a gaunt skeleton of a man covered with vermin, foul, diseased, and illiterate, is worth more than all the treasures of Paris, Rome, London, Chicago, and Buenos Aires put together" (*National Voice of Conservative Baptists,* May 1955, p. 5). Difficult to believe? Yes, but nevertheless true.

Man's capacity for fellowship with God makes his value inestimable. If a fire struck the home of a sculptor who had just finished a masterpiece, would he choose to save first that lifeless work of art, or his son asleep in the nursery, who responds lovingly to his father? Similarly, God places a unique price tag on man because he can respond to and have fellowship with Him.

Dr. Charles J. Malik, former president of the United Nations General Assembly, was asked in an interview what bearing the biblical view of God and man has on the modern controversy over human rights and duties. He answered, "Every bearing in the world. Man is made in the image of God. Man has a dignity with which he is therefore endowed by his mere humanity; he has certain natural rights and duties which stem from his being the creature of God. It is interesting to note that this whole conception of rights and of the oneness of humanity and of the universal dignity of man has arisen only within the Christian tradition" (*Christianity Today,* October 22, 1976, p. 23).

When the Christian faith became the favored religion of the Roman Empire in the days of Emperor Constantine, legislation was passed abolishing the branding of criminals and debtors on the face. Because each person is to be respected as a reflector of God's image, the early Christians uttered strong protests against the widespread practice of infanticide. Unwanted children, according to custom, were heartlessly exposed on the mountainsides to be mauled and devoured by wild beasts. Soon this evil disappeared and orphanages came into existence.

Interactionism

Among created beings, man is unique in the distinct intermeshing of his physical constitution with his psychic experience. For centuries philosophers, psychologists, and theologians have puzzled over the interactionism between body and mind. How does the sight of a steak cause saliva to flow? Or how does joy or shock cause a change in heartbeat? Or shame redden the cheek? Or music make the feet to beat? Or the mind make use of the brain as its instrument?

A preacher made the mistake one Saturday afternoon of showing two boys the Bible lesson he was planning to read Sunday morning. When he turned his back, the boys glued the pages together. Next morning the preacher read at the bottom of one page, "And Noah, when he was 120 years old, took unto himself a wife who was," and then turning the page, "300 cubits long, 50 cubits wide, and 30 cubits high, built of gopher wood and pitched within and without with pitch." Puzzled, he paused. Then he read it again. And again he paused, nonplused. Looking up, he said, "Beloved, I have read the Bible through many, many times, but this is the first time I ever read this. But I believe the Bible to be true from cover to cover. So I accept it as proof that we are fearfully and wonderfully made!" His reasoning may have been faulty, but his conclusion was accurate.

Man is marvelously made. It has been found that stress can cause ulcers, psychosomatic illness is a real thing, and depression can prolong the common cold. A happy disposition, or healthy attitude, can raise defenses against disease. The intricate inter-working of body and soul is an integral part of the way man was created.

The Age of Man

Evangelical Christianity holds that God created by supernatural means the first man as a individual being. Evangelicals are divided, however, as to the antiquity of man. How old is he?

Dr. James O. Buswell III, anthropology professor at Trinity College in Illinois, presents the two major positions as (1) those who hold that God created mankind comparatively recently, just a few thousand years ago, and (2) those who find acceptable an earlier date for Adam's creation, such as a 100,000 years ago ("Creationist Views on Human Origins" in *Christianity Today* Aug. 8, 1975, p. 4).

The first view maintains that Adam was the first man but treats the fossil remains of supposed ancient man as nonhuman animals, or fraudulent, or within the range of present man. Its proponents claim man is likely no more than 10,000 years old.

The second view resists assigning these fossils to a nonhuman type. Its supporters accept the evident humanity and geological antiquity of the data on anatomical and cultural grounds. Thus, they insist that Adam must have been created before the earliest of these specimens, likely over 100,000 years ago.

Both early and late-date views have many of the fundamentals of the faith in common. Both believe God supernaturally created Adam as the first human. Both believe man was created unique from all other creatures, not only in his discontinuity from them genetically, but also in his distinction as made in God's image. Both believe as literal the story of the Fall in the Garden of Eden. Both believe that man's creation in holiness and his subsequent Fall, are necessary prerequisites for Christ's coming to redeem.

If early and late-date Christian scholars hold so many vital doctrines in common, Dr. Buswell asks, "Why is there such decided rejection of an early or ancient date for the creation of Adam, which seems to fit the scientific date with the fewest problems? With very few exceptions, anthropologists who are creationists hold this position, namely that the cultural and anatomical remains seem both clearly ancient and clearly human."

The answer lies in the interpretation of the genealogies in Genesis 5 and 11. Because the late-date position believes the years between Adam and Abraham can be computed precisely from these chapters, its followers require Adam's creation no more than 10,000 years ago.

In response, the early-date school points out that the genealogies were not intended as chronological devices for counting the years between Adam and Abraham, thus making the age of Adam theologically irrelevant. Hebrew scholar Dr. G. Douglas Young asserts that "begat" may mean "became the ancestor of." The descendant of whom the father became the ancestor might be several steps removed down the genealogical table, thus making for unknown gaps of time. For example, when it is stated that "Seth lived an hundred and five years, and begat Enos" (Gen. 5:6), biblical usage would permit the meaning that at 105 years of age Seth became the father of a son from whose line descended Enos generations later. Thus, the genealogies would be meaningless for counting years.

A case in point is the genealogy of Christ at the beginning of the New Testament. When Jesus is said to be "the son of David, the son of Abraham" (Matt. 1:1), these progenitors, David and Abraham, are removed a thousand, and two thousand years back, respectively, from the one called their "son."

Before the turn of the century, Professors William Greene and Benjamin B. Warfield of Princeton Seminary, renowned for their loyalty to Scripture, maintained that the genealogies in Genesis should not be taken as chronology. Likewise, Francis Shaeffer asserts, "Prior to the time of Abraham, it is difficult to date the history of what we find in Scripture. It never uses these early genealogies as a chronology. It never adds up these numbers for dating" (*No Final Conflict,* InterVarsity Press, 1975, p. 39).

Further communication between the early and late-date schools may lead to clearer understanding. In the meantime, the age of man should not be made a test for orthodoxy.

Adam's Historicity

Some suggest that the first few chapters of Genesis are not history, but mythology. However, Genesis 1—11 purports to be genuine history. For centuries the church has understood these chapters as historical. Genesis 1—11 is integrated with the rest of the Book, which certainly is historical. As Francis Shaeffer points out, the phrase "these are the generations of" appears uniformly throughout the entire Book (2:4; 5:1; 6:9; 10:1; 11:10, 27; 25:12, 19; 36:1, 9; 37:2), appearing six times in the first 11 chapters, and five times from chapter 12 on, almost equally in each section.

The first genealogy in Chronicles—indisputably an historical book—begins with Adam in an unquestionably historical sense. Likewise Adam is mentioned in Christ's genealogy in Luke (3:38), and by Jude in relation to historical Enoch (v. 14).

Christ put His divine stamp of acceptance on the story of creation. Responding to a question on marriage, He asked, "Have ye not read, that He which made them at the beginning made them male and female, And said, 'For this cause shall a man leave father and mother, and shall cleave to his wife: and they twain shall be one flesh'?" (Matt. 19:4-5) Here He ties together Genesis 1 and Genesis 2, quoting them as history.

Christ also referred to the blood of Abel, Adam's son, as of a literal person (Matt. 23:35). Cain is also mentioned, without the scarcest hint that he was not an actual character (1 John 3:12; Jude 11).

The Apostle Paul several times mentions Adam as an historical personage. Adam's historicity is equated to that of Moses. Paul wrote, "Death reigned from Adam to Moses" (Rom. 5:14).

Adam's historicity is linked to even that of Christ when Paul declared that as by one man (Adam) sin entered the world . . . so by one man (Christ) came the gift of grace (see Rom. 5:12, 15). Paul also affirmed that as by man (Adam) came death, so by man (Christ) came the resurrection of the dead (see 1 Cor. 15:21-22). Paul plainly asserts, "The first man Adam was made a living soul" (15:45).

In addition, more than once Paul mentions as history the creation of Adam first, then the creation of Eve from Adam. He wrote,

"For Adam was first formed, then Eve" (1 Tim. 2:13; see also 1 Cor. 11:8-9, 12.)

It is clear that Adam's historicity cannot be laughed or sloughed off. The Bible teaches there was a first man by the name of Adam, created by God. And a first woman, named Eve, also created by God. If Adam can be demythologized, so can other important portions of Scripture.

If Jesus Christ, Lord of Glory, taught that Adam was an actual person, then we who claim to be His followers should have no problem believing it too.

3

What Was Man Like at the Beginning?

Not long ago a Missouri couple decided to take in a dirty, hungry, stray dog. Three Saturday afternoons later they left their two-year-old Margaret asleep in the car with the Irish setter, Red, standing guard while they shopped. The car's front windows were rolled down most of the way.

The father looked out frequently from a car dealer's showroom to check on his little girl. Suddenly he noticed smoke pouring from the car windows. Running toward the car, but still far from it, he saw Red jump out a front window, then immediately turn back for Margaret, who, awakened by the smoke and standing in the back seat, was swinging her arms in fright. The 75-pound dog jumped up, put his paw on the side of the car, reached his head through the smoke, grabbed Margaret's coat collar with his teeth and dragged her out the window, then pushed her away from the car. Margaret was treated for minor burns. Red suffered singed hair and a slight cut on the nose.

If a person had made that rescue, the incident would not have made the papers across the United States because humans are expected to act intelligently. Evidence overwhelmingly indicates that man is far superior to animals. Thomas Huxley, the famous zoologist and lecturer, in his book *Man's Place in Nature,* mentioned "the great gulf which intervenes between the lowest man and the highest ape in intellectual power" and "the vast intellectual chasm between the ape and man."

So great is the gap between the animal world and man that only some special act on the part of a Creator could account for it. That explanation is—"God created man in His own image" (Gen. 1:27). Or as is stated in the previous verse, man was made in God's "likeness" (1:26). Some Bible students differentiate between "image" and "likeness" by referring "image" to man's original creation, and "likeness" to that part of the "image" which man retained after the Fall. The terms, however, seem interchangeable (Gen. 5:1, 3).

Is man's likeness to God physical? Some suggest that the upright posture of man's body, plus his erect gaze, in contrast to the downward cast of animals, reflect a shadowy representation of God. The image of God in man, however, cannot refer to man's body, as it seems unlikely that man's dignity above the animals is due to his slight physiological differences or his upright stature.

Furthermore, the image cannot be physical, because God is a "spirit" and "invisible" (John 4:24; 1 Tim. 1:17; 6:16). We might wonder what organs God possesses. What is His height, weight, and color of hair and eyes? A literal interpretation of the "image" as physical simply runs counter to Scripture. The "image" must relate to the nonphysical or nonmaterial part of man's nature.

What, then, is the meaning of the image of God in man? We might propose four Rs: rule, rationality, righteousness, and relationship. These terms are suggested by the Westminster Shorter Confession which says, "God created man male and female, after his own image, in knowledge, righteousness, and holiness, with dominion over the creatures."

Man's Rule

Just as God is the all-powerful Ruler over creation, so man has been delegated authority over lower creation. Immediately after making man, God told him to subdue the earth, "and have dominion over the fish of the sea, and over the fowl of the air, and over every living thing that moveth upon the earth" (Gen.

1:28). When Noah emerged from the ark, God told him that the dread of man would be upon every creature (Gen. 9:2). The Psalmist said of man, "Thou madest him to have dominion over the works of thy hands; thou hast put all things under his feet" (8:6).

Some suggest that before the Fall Adam had power over the elements, something like that of Christ in stilling the winds and waves. Had he not sinned, scientific progress might have followed swiftly. Instead, how slowly man has extended his kingship over creation through the years!

How patiently God must have waited through the centuries for man to discover the vast resources hidden in His universe, and to utilize them. Imagine the angels of heaven, as God flashed His lightning, hoping that at last someone would discover the secrets of electricity. Then picture angels, after epochs of time, calling to each other, "See, they've finally got it!"

Think of the advances in recent years: the telephone, radio, TV, automobile, jet planes, moon landings, electronics, computers, and medical technology. Consider how miracle drugs alone have drastically reduced infant mortality and wiped out many diseases.

The mandate to subdue the earth has never been abrogated. Scientists are still free to ferret out the secrets of nature. How much more remains untouched, untapped, undreamed!

But man's technical mastery over his environment was never meant to be a tool of tyranny over others, nor was it intended for man to pollute air, water, and land without limit. To the contrary, God gave him dominion for the betterment of man and the reduction of his suffering.

Not all theologians agree that man's rule over nature is a necessary part of the meaning of God's image in man. But for many, man's dominion does reflect the image of the omnipotent Ruler.

Man's Rationality

An overenthusiastic psychology professor challenged a colleague to name a single psychological problem not referable to rats for solution. Taken by surprise, the colleague murmured something about the psychology of reading disability. (What rat can read?)

Then his mind was flooded with a myriad of things animals cannot do: compose music, build a harp, erect a cathedral, write books, laugh at comedians, make plans for three years ahead, enjoy poetry and puns, invest in the stock market, and when it crashes, contemplate suicide.

From the second century on, Christian thinkers have considered rationality a part of the image of God. Both Augustine and Calvin held this view. Adam's assignment to name the animals (Gen. 2:19), involved classification of the subordinate creatures, and seems to presuppose a rational nature. The ability to think is apparently human.

Man can go through the process of syllogism, but animals do not reason deeply, nor can they subtract, add, or divide. You wouldn't give six apples to a horse, telling him to divide them with his two equestrian friends. Animals don't go to schools. Granted, certain schools train animals to a limited extent. But no vast public school systems exist for animals as they do for our children.

In a two-section newspaper cartoon the first space pictured a monkey cage with a sign, "Please do not feed the animals." The second frame showed a monkey erasing the "not." The incongruity of a monkey showing such high intelligence gave the cartoon its comic point.

Though animals seem intelligent, especially to their owners, and though stories of animal wisdom abound, their brand of intelligence is quite inferior to that of man. They simply do not reason their way to judgments via involved logic.

Some people like to trace the similarities between the human brain and the electronic brain of giant computers. It is true that computers do many intricate problems far faster than man, but in reality the machine is at the mercy of man. Every mechanical operation is ordered by a human programmer. One electronics engineer gave his computer the acronym TOM—Thoroughly Obedient Moron.

Communication. Reason requires speech for an outlet. Because man can think, he has been endowed with an apparatus that enables him to communicate his thoughts. Man has a highly developed voice box which permits articulate speech through the utterance of involved linguistic sounds.

Thinking and speaking bear a close relationship. Someone said, "Thinking is speaking within yourself. Speaking is thinking out loud." On both counts animals are called "dumb": they do not think deeply, nor do they speak. Doubtless animals communicate on a limited level, but they do not have language, written or spoken.

Missionaries, landing on a distant shore and hearing two sets of sounds, one the chattering of people in a new language, the other the growl or squeal of animals, have translated parts of the Bible into that new human language, but never yet into the dialect of an animal.

Even mute humans can communicate by sign language, but who has ever heard of a fox on a hill waving semaphores to foxes in the valley in order to announce a chicken dinner? Even parrots do not speak. They just mimic.

A young couple courting in the living room may give junior a quarter to get him out of the living room. But they would not have to pay the family dog anything to leave, because Bozo, being without God's image, can neither understand nor report the courtship.

Inventiveness. Rationality includes the inventive faculty. Animals make wonderful things. Think of the six-sided cells of wax built by bees, or dams erected by beavers. But generation after generation of bees and beavers erect the same structures. They are unable to branch out to anything new. The bee cannot build the dam, nor the beaver the wax. Their ability is instinctive, not inventive genius.

According to the *National Geographic Magazine,* anthropologists in Zaire discovered a high level of development in chimpanzees in selecting and manipulating objects as tools. These chimps made a drinking sponge by crumpling and chewing a mass of leaves. They also used grass stalks, twigs, and sticks as primitive tools for feeding on termites and ants. Yet how elemental, minimal, and drastically inferior all this is to man's ability to operate assembly plants through sophisticated toolmaking.

True, animals do some things naturally better than people. But the human inventive faculty permits man to create that which will surpass an animal. For example, a horse can easily outrun man. But man makes a machine with enough horsepower to effortlessly outspeed the animal.

Aesthetics. God is the supreme Artist. No wonder that man, made in the divine image, is a lover of beauty, able both to create and to appreciate works of art. Rationality involves aesthetics.

Animals do not stand gazing in admiration at paintings in art galleries. Most mammals are color-blind, seeing everything in black, gray, and white. Birds are color-blind at the blue end of the spectrum but sensitive to infrared.

While human beings sing and enjoy four-part harmony, animals are unable to read a note. Dogs and cats may howl over the back fence at midnight; but we would hardly call that harmonizing soprano, tenor, alto, and bass.

Man possesses an appreciation of the beautiful which springs from the mind's response to sounds and sights in which everything seems to fall together, whether the color of a flower or the graceful swing of a professional baseball player. This sense of beauty may lie undeveloped, overwhelmed by the cares of life, but it is there, because man possesses the image of God.

Humor. Wisdom has been defined as the recognition of congruities, whereas wit is the recognition of incongruity. It takes intelligence to perceive the absurd. That's why the animals never really laugh, for they can never adjudge something incongruous. The laughing hyena simply makes noise; he is not appreciating wit.

Paul indicates that the image of God at the beginning involved rationality, when he mentions that the new man is "renewed in *knowledge after the image of Him that created him*" (Col. 3:10). The Apostle tells us in his letter to the Ephesians, however, that more than the power to reason was included in this divine image. He commands the Ephesians to "put on the new man, which *after God is created in righteousness and true holiness*" (Eph. 4:24). So morality, as well as mentality, was included in the divine image.

Man's Righteousness

When Adam came fresh from the Creator's hand, he was not morally neutral. He was holy. His nature was positively pointed to the right and opposed to the wrong. His goodness was not something accidental or added, but a quality that was stamped on him at the moment of creation. When God saw that everything was good, His view included man (Gen. 1:31). He had a capacity for righteousness, and the use of that capacity.

Though created righteous, Adam had, on the one hand, the capacity to sin and, on the other hand, the possibility of attaining a still higher righteousness in which the possibility of sinning would have been removed, like that of glorified saints in heaven. In the beginning, Adam was able to go lower or higher, depending on whether or not he passed the test of obedience God gave him in the Garden. Already possessing positive righteousness, Adam had the opportunity of increasing his holiness by means of obedience.

The tragic result is well-known. Adam failed the test and lost his righteousness, so that an unrighteous nature has been passed on to every son of Adam—even though glimmers of that original goodness still flash through today.

Man's Relationships

Made in God's likeness, man is capable of relationships that reach in three directions: toward himself, toward others, and toward God.

Self. Though man may doubt all else, he cannot doubt that he doubts. The French philosopher Descartes put it, "I think; therefore I am." Self-consciousness is unique to man. Not only does he have consciousness, but this consciousness is a unity. Man is aware of this stream of consciousness, and he perceives that he is the person who does the thinking. Though body cells may change, the same "I" who lived 10 years ago lives today, and will live throughout eternity.

A well-known Negro spiritual has caught the solemnity of the isolation of the individual soul: "Not my mother, not my sister, but it's me, O Lord, standin' in the need of prayer." We live alone in the midst of a crowd. And we die alone. Self-awareness is part of the divine image in us.

Scientists have tried to reduce awareness to a physiochemical event in the cerebral cortex, but this leaves the problem of human selfhood unsolved. Why do we use the pronouns "I," "you," and "he"? The self persists in intruding into our language. This is more than habit. It is a reflection of the impossibility of speaking without revealing the reality of our personality. A philosophy professor, asked by a student, "How do I know that I exist?", replied, "And who is asking?"

Man is able to turn upon himself reflectively and become self-conscious. One man recalls that as a small child, he one day recognized that "I was I, not someone else." That is because man is able to be both performer and spectator in relation to his own existence. An ape does not meditate on where it came from. A horse does not debate its immortality. But man knows he has a past and will have a future. He alone obeys the Socratic injunction, "Know thyself."

Along with self-consciousness, man possesses self-determination. He is capable of deliberate action. Man is a self, a conscious self, an intelligent self, and a purposeful self. Some scientists spend years trying to prove that life is purposeless. How ironic to have the goal of proving that life is without a goal!

Most importantly, self-determination is linked to man's moral nature. Adam was given the choice of eating or refraining from the forbidden fruit. He could choose the center of his affection: self or God. By virtue of the divine image, he was able to determine whether or not to follow the good.

Others. Because he was created in the likeness of Him who is Love, man was also made with the capacity for loving his fellow-men. The one word that sums up man's duty to others is love. Love to another means respect for his life (no killing), for his marriage (no adultery), for his property (no stealing), for his reputation (no lying). Paul wrote, "Love worketh no ill to his neighbor: therefore love is the fulfilling of the law" (Rom. 13:10).

Love between friends, between parents and children, between husbands and wives, all mirror God's image. Since it took both male and female to express God's likeness, perhaps companion-ship with the opposite sex, whether in the intimate relationship of marriage or in close friendship outside marriage, is necessary to reflect the full potential of the divine image in us.

God. Finally, man was made with the capacity for the worship and knowledge of God. As Genesis describes it, in the beginning Adam walked and talked with God in the Garden in the cool of the day. He wasn't described as a caveman groveling in the dust, making funny, inarticulate noises, but was an intelligent, righteous man, to whom had been given dominion over lower creatures and a right relationship with God whose image he bore. Man was in fellowship with God from the beginning. And this capacity for God, many theologians hold, is what makes a man a man. (See Gen. 2:15-16; 3:8.)

A Marred Image

When Adam sinned, however, the image of God in man was marred, or as the theologians put it—"vitiated." The original design was warped and twisted. The image, however, though scarred, was not lost.

Once a little girl saw a beautiful rainbow in the sky. Moments later she saw a varicolored smudge of oil in a mud puddle. "Look, mother," she exclaimed, "the rainbow's gone to smash." In a similar way, smudges of the heavenly image can still be seen in fallen man today.

Rule. The moral Fall of man brought a curse on the ground. Thereafter the earth yielded its fruit grudgingly. Instead of domi-nating the ground, man had to overcome it through the sweat of his brow (Gen. 3:17-19). Paul said that "the whole creation groaneth and travaileth in pain" (Rom. 8:22). The convulsions and disturbances of the ecosystem today are residual effects of man's Fall.

Man, however, still has a measure of control over nature, as we can see in the ever accelerating scientific advances. Yet man's inability to control his environment is alarmingly evident. Man is fast depleting certain of Planet Earth's elements. We are running out of food. We are overrun with people. Our biosphere is threatened with pollution. We are in danger of suffocating ourselves by contamination.

Rationality. Man also retains limited intellectual power, though his reasoning ability is tainted with fallibility. When we try to fool ourselves and others with plausible reasons to excuse our actions, we call it *rationalization,* which is a perversion of true rationality.

Righteousness. Though man also lost his righteousness in the Fall, the doctrine of total depravity does not mean that a person is completely void of kindness, or that he is completely sinful. Almost every newspaper recounts some act of decency. The lonely invalid in the infirmary with no living relative who is surprised on her birthday by nurses with a birthday cake; the girl who gives up one of her kidneys so her sister on the dialysis machine may have a chance to live; rescuers who dive into icy waters to save passengers in an airline wreck. One magazine ran a column for years, "There Are Nice People." Each month it related some good deed. This milk of human kindness is a spillover from man's original righteousness.

Conscience also points in the same direction. For several years a county commissioner in North Carolina offered his self-kicking machine to anyone who felt he should not have done something and wanted to kick himself for it. Thousands used the machine, located on Route 70. Some even formed the "Self-Kicking Club" with members scattered in every state. After the first three years a new belt was needed, plus three pairs of shoes. To work it, you just stood in front of it and moved a gadget which made the shoes revolve and kick you.

Though conscience is not an infallible guide and may become warped, dull, or calloused, this sense of right and wrong in man looks back to a day when people possessed a righteous nature.

Relationship. Since the Fall, man has been divided within himself, alienated from his fellowman, and out of tune with God. His desire for integration of personality, community with others, and worship of God, all hark back to a day when he was in right relationship in all three directions.

Fallen man reflects a lost communion with his Maker in many ways. His incurable religiosity with his need to worship something is a shadowy throwback to the day when unfallen man walked in company with God. The terrified sailors on the ship with Jonah, for example, each cried to his god.

Superstition is another evidence of man's misdirected awe of God. We find it even in civilized countries where people stand in fear of black cats, ladders, broken mirrors, and leprechauns. A stock broker received an urgent phone call from a client who said, "I'm undergoing surgery at noon. Either buy or sell 100 shares of stock. I don't want to go under the knife owning 1,300 shares!"

Can the Image Be Restored?

Through the redemptive work of Christ, man may ultimately realize the ideal for which he was created. It is possible to experience the forgiving and regenerating power of the Gospel, then grow progressively more like Jesus Christ, who Himself bore perfectly the image of God. Paul speaks of being "conformed to the image of His Son" (Rom. 8:29), of being "changed into the same image from glory to glory, even as by the Spirit of the Lord" (2 Cor. 3:18), and of someday bearing "the image of the heavenly" (1 Cor. 15:49). John says simply that we shall be "like Him" (1 John 3:2).

Michelangelo, a master sculptor, once lingered before a rough block of marble so long that his friend complained. Michelangelo replied, "There's an angel in that block and I'm going to liberate him!" Just so, the blurred image of God in man may be restored through Jesus Christ.

4

Do We All Come from Adam?

Flying saucers have been in the news for a long time now. These unidentified flying objects, called UFOs for short, have been seen in many countries. Thousands have witnessed them, including pilots, radar technicians, scientists, engineers, and ordinary citizens.

A U.S. Colonel, flying an F-84 jet on a practice mission over Japan, saw an object on his radar. Securing permission, he took off to intercept it. He described the object, hovering motionless, as "round with a center shaft of white light revolving at about five times per second." As he approached, the middle wheel accelerated in a puff of power, causing the saucer to zoom out of sight. Though he pursued with open throttle, in five seconds the object disappeared from the colonel's sight.

In Virginia a man reported a saucer, rounded at the bottom, lingering overhead at about 600 feet. After report of a UFO landing near Harrisburg, a professor from a nearby college checked the site with a Geiger counter and reported a high radiation level.

UFOs have appeared in the form of saucers, bowls, cones, eggs, and cigars. They have been tracked on radar at speeds of 10,000 miles per hour and more.

When UFO sightings were reported in the skies several summer nights in 1976 in an area of 20 to 40 miles north of New York City, attempts were made to report the sightings to the Air Force. But the Air Force replied that its investigation of UFO activity, begun in 1947, was no longer active.

An investigator, however, with the center for UFO studies in Evanston, Illinois, commented that these summer sightings were probably refracted light from stars. Other explanations for these strange phenomena are: weather balloons, meteors, airplanes, atmospheric disturbances, or optical illusions.

But some scientists believe there may be actual visitors from outer space. One said, "My opinion for some time has been that they have an extraterrestrial origin." The National Aeronautics and Space Administration recently funded the search for intelligent life in space. But is there life on other planets?

An extraordinary warning about alien intelligences elsewhere in the cosmos has been given by the noted Sir Martin Ryle, Britain's Astronomer Royal and Nobel laureate in physics. The highly respected *New York Times* commented on this warning in an editorial which assumed the existence of beings in other parts of the universe, referring to them as "intelligences," "beings," "potential visitors," and "intelligent neighbors" (*New York Times,* Nov. 22, 1976).

Ryle, worried lest fellow scientists reveal man's existence to beings on other planets, wonders if mankind should try to hide in this obscure corner of a tiny solar system. He fears that an invasion by potential visitors from Alpha Centauri, or some more distant star, would be no more merciful to us than Europeans were to American Indians only a few centuries ago.

The *Times* editorial tried to allay such fears by pointing out that the nearest intelligent beings are not likely to exist closer than hundreds of thousands of light years away. And if able to detect our existence, they would likely also be advanced in other knowledge, perchance possessing a cure for cancer and a method of controlling thermonuclear energy. Perhaps, suggests the *Times,* these alien intelligences would not prove hostile, but helpful.

Academic circles often assume today that the universe is so vast that it is likely well provided with populated stars. If true, so the argument goes, man would be so infinitesimal as to be unimportant to God, proving the absurdity of Christianity. Especially under attack is the doctrine of the Incarnation. Why would God come down to our earth, be made man for us, when we were only one in a million races sprinkled through a million globes? To believe we are so uniquely favored is the height of arrogance, critics claim.

The late C. S. Lewis, well-known professor at Cambridge University, says this objection to Christianity's main teaching could become formidable when, and if ever, we have the answer to several questions:

Do animals exist anywhere except on earth? We do not know, and we may never know. If they do exist elsewhere, do they have rational, moral souls which possess not only the faculty of abstraction, but also the power of doing good? If such creatures don't exist anywhere else, then man is unique, and the special treatment given him through the Incarnation need not be considered strange.

Another important question is—if another spiritual species exists, has it sinned? To criticize Christianity because of the Incarnation is to assume the Fall of other creatures whose mere existence is also assumed.

Still another question, if other intelligences exist elsewhere and have sinned, has redemption been refused them? Could not Christ have become incarnate in other worlds and suffered so as to save races other than ours? Or is man the only lost sheep for whom the Shepherd came seeking?

Lewis then asks a final question that almost bowls us over. Is it certain that only one way of salvation exists? If there were different kinds of Falls in different kinds of worlds, perhaps the Great Physician applied different remedies, so that a fallen race could have been rescued apart from Bethlehem and Calvary.

Lewis sums up his thoughts about rational life on other planets in this way:

> The mere existence of these creatures would not raise a problem. After that, we still need to know that they are fallen; then, that they have not been, or will not

be, redeemed in the mode we know; and then, that no other mode is possible. I think a Christian is sitting pretty if his faith never encounters more formidable difficulties than these conjectural phantoms. If I remember rightly, St. Augustine raised a question about the theological position of satyrs, monopods, and other semihuman creatures. He decided it could wait till we knew there were any. So can this (*The World's Last Night,* Harcourt, Brace and Jovanovich, 1960, pp. 91-92).

One thing is certain—if other beings exist elsewhere, they cannot trace their ancestry to Adam. But on earth every last one of us belongs to the same family. Adam is the father of us all.

Unity of the Human Race

Corporal Joe Green of Louisiana claimed direct descent from Adam and Eve and had a document to prove it. To scoffing barrack mates he produced a birth certificate which read, "Joseph Green, born to Eve and Adam Green."

Every person's ancestry traces back to a single pair, the Adam and Eve of the Garden of Eden. Eve was so named because she was the mother of all that were ever to live (Gen. 3:20). The line came down through Noah. "And the sons of Noah, that went forth of the ark, were Shem, and Ham, and Japheth. *. . .* These are the three sons of Noah; and of them was the whole earth overspread" (Gen. 9:18-19). This natural brotherhood, to be distinguished from the spiritual brotherhood of the family of God, constitutes a ground for kind treatment of all our fellowmen.

Incidentally, the question of where Cain got his wife is logically answered this way: He likely married a sister, which would not be considered incest in that situation.

No nation on the face of the earth can today crawl into its shell or hide its head in the sand and thus detach itself from other nations. After a round-the-world trip a generation ago, a presidential aspirant, Wendell Willkie, wrote a book titled, *One World.* He pointed out that a shrinking world has removed the United States from a position of isolation into a global community of nations whose troubles are also our troubles. But long before Willkie propounded his one-world thesis, the Bible taught the concept of the unity of the human race.

Today, an ever smaller world, made so by jet travel and TV satellites, creates a problem. Unlike the parents of an ornery boy who bought him a bike so he could spread his meanness out from his home and street to the entire neighborhood, we are fast running out of global space in which to exercise our depravity. Though we are becoming one vast neighborhood, we are becoming less neighborly. Someone punned, "That's no glo-bal-oney, for in the past half-century we have suffered two world wars."

The unity of the human race in our one world is shown in many ways.

Historically. Three hundred miles south of the ruins of Babylon reads a sign, "Garden of Eden." Though no one knows where the real Garden was located, many students of the origins of man believe that the history of nations points to a common origin and ancestry through successive emigrations from Asia.

Interestingly, the Euphrates (on which Babylon is located) and the Tigris (Hiddekel), which flows not far away, are both mentioned in connection with Eden (Gen. 2:14).

Linguistically. Many philologists believe that all the principal languages of the world have a common origin. Years ago an article in *Time* magazine demonstrated resemblances of the letters of the alphabet in Greek, Hebrew, Chinese, and Assyrian ("Letters from Heaven," *Time*, April 4, 1955, pp. 43-44).

The two major families of languages, Semitic and Indo-European, reflect similarities. Note the kinship of the word *father* in various tongues: Latin, *pater;* Danish, *vader;* Swedish, *fader;* German, *vater;* French, *pere*. Names ending in *sen* or *son* mean "son of." The equivalent in Irish is *o*—such as O'Brien—while in German and Dutch, it is *van*, or *von*, and in French *de*. Do not the similarities of languages suggest some common origin? Certainly, the Bible indicates the world had a common language till Babel (Gen. 11:1).

Physically. The physiological structure of the human body implies that we all belong to one species. Racial peculiarities are minimal compared to basic, overall similarities. A book written on anatomy by a Japanese doctor would apply to North Americans. Generally, all peoples have the same number of bones, same brain and nervous systems, same distribution of blood vessels, same organs for breathing and digestion, same heart design, same four types of blood, so that transfusion from an African to a Spaniard will work. God "hath made of one blood all nations of men for to dwell on all the face of the earth" (Acts 17:26). A United Nations blood bank, created for use in the Korean War, contained blood from many countries.

All people everywhere eat, thirst, sleep, shed tears, and cohabit with fertility. No race is superior. A Britisher, lecturing in an African missionary college, took the line that the weight and structure of a black African's brain rendered it incapable of being developed by higher education. Thinking his audience exclusively European, he was surprised in the question-and-answer period when a tall, ebony man rose to thank the lecturer for his interesting talk. Then this black college teacher added, "You know, it reminded me of what I read last night in a volume of Cicero's letters. In this letter, written to his friend Atticus, a millionaire employer of slave labor, Cicero [a second century Roman statesman] remarks that of all his slaves the British were the most stupid." Then the black man commented wryly, "How you have come on!"

Psychologically. A textbook on psychology would describe human nature the world around. All nationalities have the same emotions, instincts, and passions. Their maxims and traditions are strikingly similar. Worldwide, children like to play. Not only in America, but in Japan and China and France, people suffer nervous breakdowns. Everywhere, whether in Botswana or Italy, people love their families.

Before Pearl Harbor, Madame Chiang Kai-shek flew to Hong Kong to have her teeth attended to by an American dentist. The trip was unofficial and without fanfare, though the British newspaper did mention that the Generalissimo's wife was a visitor to the city.

After a few days both the Governor's house and Madame's

party were agitated. Why? Because any visitor to Hong Kong was supposed to make a visit to the Governor. Since it was impossible for the Governor to see every visitor, the visitor was supposed to sign the Governor's guestbook. Then it was up to the Governor to make the next move. If the visitor was important enough, he might soon receive an invitation to dine at the Governor's residence. Theoretically, the only persons who would not be expected to visit the Governor were those so important that the Governor would be expected to pay respect to them.

The reason for agitation in this case—who was more important, Madame Chiang Kai-shek or the Governor? The situation was solved by mutual inactivity. Madame didn't sign, nor did the Governor invite. So both kept their pride. It isn't just the Chinese who like to save face. Pride is a universal trait.

Spiritually. The oneness of the human race is shown by the universality of sin. Adam's sinful nature has been passed on to the entire race. Unlike mankind, not all angels are sinful, for they were created separately, fell individually, and are not united organically. But all humans sin.

Where Does the Soul Come From?

If every member of the race can trace his ancestry back to Adam, the question is often asked—where does our soul come from? Three major views have been set forth to explain the origin of the soul:

(1) *preexistentialism*, which teaches the soul existed previously in another body;

(2) *creationism*, which says that God creates each individual soul at conception, or at birth, or sometime between;

(3) *traducianism*, which holds that the soul is passed down from parents.

Preexistentialism was held by Origen, the early Christian leader in Alexandria, to justify the wide disparity of conditions in which people enter our world. The same view was espoused by Philo, the Jewish philosopher, to explain the soul's imprisonment in the body. Four centuries before Christ, Plato taught the preexistence of the soul to account for the existence of ideas not derived from sense.

But preexistentialism has a number of weaknesses: It has no Scripture to support it, makes the body accidental, removes the distinction between men and angels, contradicts the creation account, destroys the unity of the human race as all coming from Adam, finds no support in our consciousness, and does away with responsibility for deeds done in one's own exclusive body. As a consequence, evangelical theologians hold to either creationism or traducianism. Both these views, however, have their own points and problems.

Creationism is consistent with Scripture which pictures souls coming from God (Isa. 57:16; Ecc. 12:7; Heb. 12:9). But could not these verses refer to mediate creation through parents (traducianism), as well as immediately by God? Creationism, however, seems more consistent with the indivisibility of the soul, for if the soul comes from the parents, then it would seem to be a combination or synthesis of two souls, those of both mother and father.

On the other hand, creationism seems to make God the author of our depraved tendencies, forgets that a person's psychological traits, as well as his physical ones, come from parents, and seems out of harmony with God's present method of working mediately instead of immediately.

Traducianism fits those Bible verses which tell of God's command to man to propagate, which speak of God ceasing from creation after making man, and which refer to one's descendents as being in "the loins" of a progenitor (Gen. 1:28; 2:2; 46:26; Heb. 7:9-10). Could this be the reason we speak of the ongoing of the race as procreation, not creation?

Traducianism also seems to provide the best explanation for the inheritance of moral depravity, for "that which is born of the flesh is flesh" (John 3:6). The idea that the soul has a parental origin also seems to find support in Genesis 5 which says, "And Adam lived an hundred and thirty years, and begat a son in his own likeness, after his image; and called his name Seth" (5:3).

A strong objection to this view appears when it is applied to

Christ. If true, would not Christ have been born with a sinful soul? But could not the overshadowing of Mary by the Holy Spirit (Luke 1:35) have kept the baby holy from the first moment of conception?

Universals and the Unity of the Race

Universality of sin. Humans everywhere sin. Men murder in South America. A sign on a Hong Kong ferry reads, "Beware of pickpockets." Japanese husbands are guilty of adultery. Racial strife breaks out in Malaysia. Violence stalks the United States. Prostitution flourishes in the Philippines. No member of the human race is exempt from sinning.

Universality of death. Because of sin, "death passed upon all men" (Rom. 5:12). Death has a key to every home, whether on boulevard or bowery. Every newspaper carries its advertisement. Every tombstone is its pulpit. To stress the universality of death, a hearse once bore the license plate: U-2.

Universal need. All men need the Saviour because hanging over the head of every person is the penalty of sin, which is a lost eternity. As through Adam all become lost, so all who link themselves to Christ by faith will be saved. The Second Adam joined Himself to our sinful race that He might start a righteous family.

Universal offer of pardon. The Great Commission clearly commands, "Go ye into all the world and preach the Gospel to every creature" (Mark 16:15). This offer is possible because, "God so loved the world." Also, because Christ "is the propitiation for our sins: and not for ours only, but also for the sins of the whole world" (1 John 2:2).

Man everywhere is religious, trying somehow to rightly relate himself to the deity he has offended. But man can never be satisfied till he hears and responds to the message of the Lamb of God who takes away the sin, the restlessness, the guilt, and the alienation of the human heart, worldwide.

Universal praise. A few years ago, through the wonders of TV and satellites, millions of people from over 120 countries saw the first man step onto the moon. Someday a multitude which no man can number will sing to the Lord Jesus Christ, the Second

Adam, "Thou art worthy . . . for Thou wast slain, and has redeemed us to God by Thy blood out of every kindred, and tongue, and people, and nation" (Rev. 5:9).

5

Can We Believe the Story of Adam and Eve?

Since the turn of the century we have had two World Wars plus the costly Korean and Vietnam battles, to say nothing of numerous regional conflicts.

Many of our cities are unsafe at night. Several VIPs have been assassinated. A Columbia University professor was bludgeoned to death by a teenage gang. A young woman was repeatedly and fatally stabbed in New York City while nearly 40 bystanders turned a deaf ear to her cries for help.

If at the beginning man was created in the image of God, with rationality and righteousness, how do we account for the moral mess in which we find the world today? Why has man through history been at odds with himself, alienated from his fellowman, and at enmity with God? Why in this day of scientific achievement, with all its curative powers, is man the most miserable, unfulfilled, and frustrated of God's creation? The answer is that man fell from the holy estate he enjoyed at the beginning.

The Importance of Genesis 3
Genesis 3 contains important teaching on major Christian doctrines: God's holiness and grace, Satan, judgment, salvation, prophecy, angels, and Christ, "the seed of the woman." But most

crucial, the chapter tells how sin, already in the universe because of Satan, entered the human stream.

When you buy an appliance, you usually receive a book of directions which tells how to maintain the machine's smooth operation. Our Maker has given us a book of directions to explain man's behavior. This manual tells how man lived righteously when he came fresh from the Creator's hands; but then he ran counter to his Creator's will, thus getting himself out of kilter and causing his present disjointed behavior. Man's rebellion has left a trail of sorrow, crime, and death. Sin has dug millions of graves. It has caused the earth to echo with the groans of those who are afflicted and burdened. It has toppled men from high positions, and buried empires in the dust of oblivion. Genesis 3 provides the answer to the eternal "why" of centuries of evil.

If this vital chapter were ripped from the Bible, we would be left without adequate explanation of man's depravity. Also, the rest of the Bible would seem unnecessary, for Scripture from this point on deals with God's plan of salvation from sin.

Incidentally, many cultures contain the clouded memory of a lost Eden. This recurring theme in their literature points back to a golden age, which man once enjoyed and for which he seems to subconsciously long. Somehow man cannot forget this past utopia. As Chad Walsh of Beloit College puts it, "We are haunted by memories of the original Garden and that lost innocence. In our heart of hearts, we know that our race has not always lived in . . . a world shot through with oppression, misunderstanding, meaninglessness, tragedy, cruelty, individual and collective insanity; a world haphazardly redeemed by some moments and deeds of niggardly virtue and grudging magnanimity, and fugitive instants of compassion and love. It was not always so. . . . The poor thing we commonly call our 'human nature' was not our first nature; it is a pathological condition" (*From Utopia to Nightmare,* Harper and Row, 1962, p. 30).

The Circumstances of the Fall

Place. The locale of man's initial rebellion against God was the Garden of Eden. Placed in a paradise, man was on probation.

Nature of the test. How easy God made the test! Man was told he could eat of every tree of the Garden, except one. God didn't say, "You may eat from only one tree, but all the others you must stay away from." God generously told Adam, "You may eat of all the trees. Just abstain from one." One small prohibition that was in a Garden full of permissible fruit.

Purpose of the test. Everything turned on the test of wills. The fruit would show whether man would submit to God, or cut loose from God's lordship. The temptation boiled down to, "Don't listen to God. Do what *you* want. Don't let anyone stand in your way and dictate to you." Would man do what *God* created him to do? Or would man do what *he* chose to do? Would man obey God's will, or would man exalt his will above God's?

Contrary to popular opinion, the forbidden fruit was not likely an apple. Years ago an organization that offered $1,000 to anyone proving a scientific error in the Bible was challenged with this argument: Apples do not grow in the Mesopotamia area. Since the Garden of Eden was in the Mesopotamia area, Adam could not have eaten the apple, and the Bible must be scientifically wrong. The organization asked the challenger to produce chapter and verse which stated the forbidden fruit was an apple, but he was unable to do so. A wit once observed that the trouble was not the apple on the tree but the "pair" on the ground.

The forbidden fruit was from "the tree of the knowledge of good and evil" (Gen. 2:17). The result of man's testing would show whether his future would be good or evil. By yielding to sin, man would gain the ability to distinguish between good and evil, but through the wrong channel of personal experience. The right way was through the resistance of temptation. This would lead to the attainment of the proper discernment between good and evil. Jesus Christ, who certainly knew how to tell good from evil, never had to experience evil in order to gain this knowledge.

Duration of the probation. The testing period was to be limited. Otherwise man would have been forever faced with the unsettling possibility of a Fall, but never the glorious attainment of a state of final security.

A time span was necessary to give man an opportunity to be

established in holiness. Though man had a righteous nature at the beginning, he did not then possess a righteous character. Character develops only as we make successive choices for the good. The boy who successfully resists a temptation to steal, gains strength to withstand his next urge to dishonesty. After a continuous, or nearly continuous set of victories, he develops an honest character. Alternate choice makes character possible. That is why Adam, created with the possibility of character, but not yet with character, needed time to be established in holiness.

Once established, however, at some point God would have declared the probation over, and granted Adam the assured blessedness of a higher condition in which the possibility of sinning would have been removed. Does not the Christian envision a time (in heaven) when even the possibility of his sinning is past? We don't hope to return to the condition of Adam before the Fall, but to an entrance into a far higher condition, which would have been Adam's experience had he passed the probation period successfully.

Steps to the Fall

The enticer. Satan, a personal, malicious being, appearing under the guise of a serpent, tempted Eve. The Apostle Paul tells us that the serpent beguiled Eve through his subtilty (2 Cor. 11:3). John also identifies the devil with a serpent when he refers to the tempter as "that old serpent, which is the Devil, and Satan" (Rev. 20:2).

How fitting for Satan to be compared to a serpent. Like a snake, the devil moves quietly, stealthily, and strikes without warning. The steps in the devil's strategy show striking similarities to the ways he works today.

An indirect approach. Satan did not approach Adam directly, but stayed several steps from his prey. Satan used a serpent to approach Eve, who then reached Adam.

Incidentally, an effective way of reaching a person's heart is through someone he loves. Satan's use of Eve to tempt Adam wasn't the last time the devil got to someone through a wife or close companion.

Moreover, the evil one found the woman when she was alone. Because the prohibition was given Adam before Eve's creation, perhaps the devil thought a secondhand warning would be less of a deterrent, making her more susceptible to temptation (Gen. 2:16-17).

Eve's willingness to listen. Instead of resisting the devil, Eve took the chance to join in dialogue with him. C. S. Lewis in his book, *Perelandra,* suggests that Eve was finally worn down by her willingness to listen to what he had to say about sin and what it would do or not do to her. She wanted to be mature, tolerant, and fair to the devil. But her self-confidence carried her too far.

Insinuation against God's goodness. The devil asked, "Yea, hath God said, 'Ye shall not eat of every tree of the garden'?" (Gen. 3:1) With a sneer he implied, "How loving is a god that would make such a prohibition? Is he keeping something from you which you would enjoy?"

Eve seemed to follow this lead by adding to God's original command, *"neither shall ye touch it"* (Gen. 3:3). Petulantly, she betrayed a slight suspicion that perhaps God was holding something back on her, like a child who, justifiably refused something by a parent, retorts, "You never give me anything!" Eve accepted Satan's insinuation to the extent that she wondered why God established limits in Paradise.

Instilling doubt. Satan's next trick was to deny God's Word, "Ye shall not surely die" (3:4). This was a half-truth, for they would not die physically for a while. But the half-lie was that they would die spiritually the moment they sinned. Though Satan dangled the bait of no immediate payoff, the wages would ultimately be paid.

The delay in the penalty for sin enables the sinner to indulge in wrong, even continue in it for a while, before the axe falls.

Appeal to pride. Satan followed his advantage by saying, "Your eyes shall be opened, and ye shall be as gods, knowing good and evil" (3:5). But Adam was already "in the know" because God had told him the truth about what would happen.

Too often people don't want to accept God's verdict but must learn the hard way, through personal experience. Addison H. Leitch, the late professor of philosophy at Gordon-Conwell Seminary, once said:

> It is this appeal to sophistication which is the trap for so many of us, especially young people. We must experiment with sin for fear we are somehow missing something. Missing what? The destroyer! We seem to sense this in something like the use of dope where the reaction time is brief and destructiveness is immediately evident. But here the "timing" gets interlocked with our problem, when, in so many cases we can enjoy the taste of sin, its air of sophisticated intelligence (and pride), and really find "nothing too harmful." Here is the temptation of our knowledge as against God's knowledge, e.g., sophistication as against wisdom. God knows us, He knows what sin is, He knows what sin will do to us; thus His most solemn warnings. When man sins anyway, there is no going back to live as if the sin had not been committed. It is like the breaking of a beautiful vase, or the marring of a work of art; we can never pretend that things are just the same again (*Interpreting Basic Theology,* Channel Press, 1961, pp. 64-65).

Appeal to innocent appetites. "The woman saw that the tree was good for food, and that it was pleasant to the eyes" (3:6). Though things may look good in and of themselves, we are not to partake of them, if God has forbidden them. What may be good *per se* may not be good when taken in disobedience. Nothing was wrong in the making of stones into bread, but Jesus knew that this particular act would display defiant independence of His Father's will, and thus make an act, innocent in itself, evil. Eve was blinded to such consequences.

The overt act. Eve yielded to her desires. She did not sin in being tempted, but in yielding to temptation. Since sin may be in our thought life before an actual deed, it is not always easy to determine just when temptation becomes sin. Eve had been sliding downward from the moment she began giving credence to the tempter's lures. The overt act followed the thought easily.

Notice how the areas of appeal coincide with those described by John (1 John 2:16). Eve saw that the tree was:

good for food	—the lust of the flesh
pleasant to the eyes	—the lust of the eyes
to be desired to make one wise	—the pride of life

Sharing of sin. Immediately, Eve involved Adam in her sin. Like misery, sin loves company. Not content to indulge alone, sinners try to involve others in their misdeeds. Do we think that our sin will be hidden by the acts of others? In fact, guilt cannot be reduced by sharing it with another. Every man must give an account of his own sins.

Adam apparently knew what he was doing when he ate. An old pun makes the point. For one hour a preacher emphasized Eve's blame, repeating that she ate the fruit first and thus created the world's mess. At the end of the service a lady asked him, "What was the phone number in the Garden of Eden?" When the preacher looked puzzled, she replied, "Adam 8-1-2" (ate-one-too).

The Results of the Fall

The moment our first parents disobeyed God they "fell," that is, they lost their original righteousness. We will discuss the disastrous results of the Fall on the entire human race in the following chapter. At this point we ought to notice the consequences which affected Adam and Eve immediately, and which in many ways find their counterpart in every sinner throughout history. The devil promised Eve that they would find out the score. And they surely did!

Shame. The first consequence of the Fall was the feeling of shame that Adam and Eve experienced. A newspaper picture of two youths arrested for robbery showed them holding their arms over their faces. Their sense of shame reflects the disgrace Adam and Eve felt when, coming to know sin experientially, they realized their nakedness and clothed themselves (3:7). How easily people blush when caught in a lie. Shame is the result of the Fall.

Fear. The shame that Adam and Eve felt was followed by fear.

In the cool of the day the Lord came seeking Adam and Eve. The first reference to fear in the Bible can be detected in Adam's answer to the Lord when He asked him why he hid; "I heard Thy voice in the garden, and I was afraid" (3:8-10).

People have been known to "get religion" during storms. The Roman Emperor Augustus used to hide in a cellar in a thunderstorm, while Emperor Caligula took refuge under a bed. Fear is a common human response to the unknown or an uncertain situation.

Back in 1938 Orson Welles' radio production of H. G. Wells' *War of the Worlds* terrified people all over America. Some years later a tribute to him in the form of a fictional radio play, which described an "antiaircraft defense ray which destroyed all matter and which had gotten out of control and was sucking up the earth's supply of air," sent many running from their homes in South Carolina. During an earthquake in California a call from the eighth floor to the hotel's desk asked for a Bible to be sent up. "But you have one in the room," the clerk answered. "That's true," said the person calling, "but my husband is reading it, and I want a copy for myself."

Discord. A third consequence of the Fall was discord. One computer was described as human because when it made a mistake it blamed another computer. When God confronted Adam with his sin, he saddled Eve with the responsibility. "The woman whom Thou gavest to be with me, she gave me of the tree, and I did eat" (3:12). Adam even hinted God was partly at fault, "the woman *Thou* gavest me." Eve, blamed by Adam, passed the buck, "The serpent beguiled me" (3:13).

How human to shrug the blame off on someone else! "Everybody's doing it." "I'm not responsible; my parents didn't love me." "My wife drove me to it. She doesn't understand me." "I was brought up in the wrong neighborhood."

Incidentally, this wasn't the last time sin caused discord in the first family. Later, malice on the part of Adam and Eve's son Cain, led to the murder of his brother, Abel.

The three hardest words to say are, "I have sinned." From the Fall to this day, sin struggles to excuse itself.

Death. Another result of the Fall was death as judgment for eating the forbidden fruit. "In the day that thou eatest thereof thou shalt surely die" (Gen. 2:17). Spiritual death came at the moment of rebellion; physical death followed years later.

Physical death was not merely a biological event; it was a penalty decreed by God. Had Adam not sinned, he would not have died. Paul seems to teach this when he says that "By one man sin entered into the world, and death by sin; and so death passed upon all men, for that all have sinned; . . . by one man's offense death reigned by one" (Rom. 5:12, 17).

Just as some day, at the second coming of Christ, a generation of believers will not die but have their bodies transformed without passing through any dissolution between body and soul in death, so God would have preserved Adam from physical death, had he not sinned. As J. Gresham Machen says, "The Bible seems rather clearly to teach that death, even physical death, was the penalty of sin, and that life, even physical life, would have been the result of obedience" (*The Christian View of Man,* Eerdmans, 1947, p. 185).

Separation. A fifth consequence of the Fall was that Adam and Eve were expelled from Paradise and all its joys. "The Lord God sent him forth from the Garden of Eden. . . . So He drove out the man; and He placed at the east of the Garden of Eden Cherubims, and a flashing sword which turned every way, to keep the way of the tree of life" (3:23-24).

Sin separates. It divides nations, churches, families; it puts men behind prison bars, removing them from loved ones and society. Adam lost Paradise, not only for himself, but for his posterity. For when Adam's children were born, they were born outside the Garden.

The Second Adam Met the Test

Adam's sin did not surprise God. He permitted man to fall in a way that preserved to the full man's personal freedom and responsibility. God is not the author of sin. Yet we admit the eternal mystery of evil. While acknowledging our need to trust God alone for the answer to this seemingly insoluble riddle, we do find in

Scripture the answer to a much more crucial question, namely, "What is the remedy for sin?"

Picture a man trapped on the fifth floor of a burning building with no escape except by leaping into a net which the firemen are holding ready. Imagine the trapped man hollering down, "I will not jump until you give me a satisfactory explanation of how the fire started, and where, and why it spread so quickly, and why fire extinguishers weren't successful. Until you come up with a good answer, I'm staying right here!"

Just so, the question as to why God allowed sin to enter the world is comparatively unimportant, even irrelevant, as we find ourselves in a lost condition, headed for eternal perdition. The critical question is, "What is the remedy for sin?"

The remedy is the Second Adam. God did not abandon Adam when he sinned. Indeed God came seeking man. Other religions begin with man seeking after God. Only the Bible presents a God who searches for man. "The Lord God called unto Adam, 'Where art thou?'" (3:9) The rest of the Bible records the outworking of God's plan to bring man back into fellowship with Himself. The last chapter of the Bible has man restored to a new Paradise (Rev. 22:1-3).

The first Adam dragged the race down. The second Adam lifted the believing race up. As by one man came sin and death, so by one man came righteousness and life. In Adam all die; in Christ shall all live (Rom. 5:12-19; 1 Cor. 15:22).

How significant that the Second Adam conquered the very same temptations which felled the first Adam. Satan tempted Christ with the lust of the flesh ("Make these stones into bread"), the lust of the eye ("See all these kingdoms which, if You bow to me, will be Yours"), and the pride of life ("Jump from the temple pinnacle for angels will bear You up—You're important"). Christ was victor in every area (Luke 4:1-13).

Christ's redemption aims to transform man's selfish, rebellious nature into the divine image in which he was originally created. To all who repent of their waywardness God grants forgiveness and new life. The Paradise lost through Adam is restored through the reconciling Christ.

6

What Is Sin?

When a mysterious disease killed more than 20 people and sickened another 100, right after the American Legion Convention in Philadelphia in 1976, an uneasy anxiety gripped the area. When the conventionnaires returned home, relatives and friends feared contamination. Congress almost immediately passed a bill authorizing nationwide immunization against the swine flu, hoping to avert an epidemic.

Oldtimers recalled the 1918 flu epidemic which, in a few months, took a worldwide toll of more than 21 million people, a figure exceeding the total number of deaths, military and civilian, in both World Wars I and II.

Called the greatest plague of modern times, the 1918 flu pandemic had only two rivals in all recorded history, the plague of A.D. 542 and the Black Death of the 14th century. All three epidemics hit without warning, killed suddenly, spread explosively, then just as quickly vanished.

The greatest of all human plagues, however, is sin. This disease began with Adam, has infected every member of the race (except Christ), dooms unless treated by the one and only remedy, shows no sign of abatement, and will be with us until the day the Saviour banishes pain, tears, and death.

What Is Sin?

A number of years ago the Finnish Broadcasting Company offered prizes to those listing the most synonyms for certain words. A working man in North Finland won an award for submitting 747 synonyms for drunkenness. A man serving a prison sentence came in second with 678. The same prisoner won a prize for listing 170 synonyms for stealing. Another man knew 203 for lying. This rich vocabulary for each of these sins may spring from man's tendency to avoid calling his misdeeds by the name God has put on them—sin.

The sociologist calls sin "cultural lag."

The psychiatrist terms it "emotional behavior."

The philosopher names it "irrational thinking."

The humanist excuses it as "human weakness."

The Marxist defines it as "class struggle."

The psychologist explains it in terms of a "psychophysical mechanism" which leaves the soul helpless, in the control of genes and gastric juices.

The Freudian speaks of the "id."

A Congressman refers to his immoral relationship with his secretary as "a bit of foolishness."

The layman says it's just plain "cussedness."

The criminologist writes it off as "antisocial conduct."

Some philosophers regard sin as the limitation of being—absolute evil is nothingness. But the Bible sees sin as a positive reality.

Some say the source of sin resides in the body. But a sensuous origin cannot account for some of the worst sins—pride, envy, and greed, which pertain to the soul. When the Bible speaks of the flesh fighting the spirit, "flesh" refers to our sinful nature, not to our body.

The association of sin with the body *per se* is usually traceable to a dualistic theory which teaches the existence of two eternal principles, one of evil, the other of good. The Bible, however, says that God is the only eternal being.

Another erroneous concept explains sin as the opposition of man's lower tendencies to a gradually developing moral consciousness. Evil is, supposedly, good in the making. As man evolves toward perfection, his brute inheritance will slowly fade away like a vestigial remnant. But man is not progressing toward perfection.

Some cults make sin an illusion of the mortal mind, affirming that evil does not exist. A good answer to that view would be the words of a cemetery gardener who, coming across a gravestone with this inscription, "Not dead, but sleeping," scratched his head reflectively, then remarked, "He isn't fooling anybody but himself."

What, then, is sin? The Westminster Shorter Catechism defines it "as any want (lack) of conformity unto, or transgression of, the law of God."

Sin is a specific kind of evil. Not physical evil like sickness or an earthquake, but moral evil committed by a rational creature.

Sin has positive character, making impossible the position of the naturalist who says human nature is morally neutral. John wrote, "Sin is the transgression of the law" (1 John 3:4). Sin is failure to conform to the divine standard of right and wrong. A word for sin in both Hebrew and Greek means "missing the mark." To fail to hit the bull's-eye of righteousness is to sin.

Sins can be divided into those of omission and those of commission. The priest and Levite who failed to show kindness to the wounded Jew in Jesus' parable of the Good Samaritan were as guilty of wrongdoing as the robbers who beat him. "To him that knoweth to do good, and doeth it not, to him it is sin" (James 4:17).

Sin is not merely an act, but a state or condition. Jesus pointed out where sins begin; "For out of the heart proceed evil thoughts, murders, adulteries, fornications, thefts, false witness, blasphemies" (Matt. 15:19).

Sin, therefore, must be differentiated from *sins.* Some hold that selfishness is the basic principle of sin. Others consider the essence of sin to be pride, or unbelief, or world-love, or enmity to God. But sin needs to be traced back to its ultimate source. *Sin* belongs to the nature of man; *sins* are the outward manifestation of that inward sinful nature. Our predicament is reflected in the message scribbled over a nonworking clock, "Don't blame my hands; the trouble lies deeper."

A wolf cub, reared in a domestic atmosphere, seemed tame enough. But one day the growing animal's real nature broke out with a devastating attack on the other animals in the barn. This act didn't make him a wolf. He acted this way because he was already a wolf. We are not sinners because we sin; we sin because we are sinners.

Back in 1950 the Hayden Planetarium was only kidding when it offered to take reservations for trips to the moon and other planets. The Planetarium said jokingly that it would turn the reservations over to the first interplanetary travel agency, when and if organized. Those wishing to make reservations were to check their choice, in order of their distance, ranging from the nine and one-half hour trip to the moon, 238,000 miles away, or to Venus, or to Mars, or to Jupiter, or to Saturn, 790 million miles away which would take over three and one-half years. Though the Planetarium's "Passenger Briefing" warned that these places might be very inhospitable to human life, more than 18,000 reservations or requests for information flooded the Planetarium within a few weeks. One man wanted to start a skating rink on Venus. A New York fur broker asked about trading rights.

Later in 1965, Pan American World Airlines began accepting reservations for the first commercial rocket flight to the moon, but had only 200 applications before the Apollo 8 mission, after which 25,000 reservations poured in.

Trans World Airlines also began accepting reservations for their first flight. The *New York Times* reported that though TWA's figures were not as numerous, they were mounting rapidly. The *Times* also reported that fare rates, based on the then current 6¢ a mile, would make the moon trip cost $14,000 one way (*New York Times,* July 21, 1969, p. 52).

A psychologist, making a study of this widespread wish to travel to the moon, concluded that most people did not think the offers a joke, and just wanted to escape "this sorry earth." One woman commented on her reservation request, "I just want to go somewhere where it is nice and peaceful, safe and secure."

But, wherever man goes, he cannot escape himself. If he should ever be able to escape the evils of this world and start a colony on the moon, he would eventually make a similar mess up there because he would have taken his sinful nature along.

> If man should ever reach the moon,
> There's one thing that is clear;
> He'll ruin everything up there,
> Just like he has down here.
> —Author unknown

This pervasive evil in the heart of man is called "original sin."

The Meaning of Original Sin

Toward the close of World War II, a lady was being shown around a bombed-out city in Europe. As she stood, stunned by the sight of a pile of half-buried corpses, and nauseated by the stench of decay, her guide remarked, "This is what original sin has done." She retorted, "Need you bring in that horrible doctrine?" He replied, "Madam, anything so horrible as this requires a horrible explanation."

Original sin simply means that every person enters the world a sinner, without righteousness, possessing a corrupt nature out of which all individual transgressions proceed.

Our inward, sinful nature is the root or *origin* from which all outward sins spring. Sin inheres in each person's nature from the *origin* of life, and is not learned by imitation. Sin goes back to the *origin* of the human race, Adam and Eve.

The inherent sinfulness of man is taken for granted by the writers of the New Testament. Christ's words presuppose this view of human nature, "If ye then, being evil, know how to give good gifts unto your children . . ." (Matt. 7:11).

Though we live in a seemingly advanced state of civilization, immediately below the veneer lie our lower passions, so ready to erupt in a variety of unkind and cruel ways.

Perhaps the most graphic example of man's inhumanity to man in our century was the holocaust of the Nazi concentration camps. A few years ago 5,000 survivors of Auschwitz held a reunion in a New York City hotel. Clusters of men shouted glad greetings, or embraced with tears. Every man in the room had endured unimaginable suffering and degradation as a slave laborer. Back in early 1945 they had been marched west, ahead of the onrushing Soviet armies. Most then weighed 100 pounds or less, their heads shaved, their shrunken, cadaverous bodies garbed in the blue and white striped uniform of the camp.

At their reunion the men displayed photographs of how they looked in 1945. They pulled up their sleeves to display the registration number tattooed in blue on their left forearms. One man carried a little box which contained the ashes of an unknown prisoner who had been gassed, then cremated. How else can we explain such atrocities apart from the doctrine of original sin?

How ironical that while religious liberals and humanists are busy denying original sin, the doctrine is being reaffirmed in the realm of psychoanalysis. What our modern world wouldn't take from Augustine and Luther, it has had to take from Freud. While refusing to use such terminology as "original sin" and "total depravity," psychoanalysts have had to admit the reality of that for which such terms stand.

Someone has observed that a psychiatrist and a coal miner have a great deal in common. The psychiatrist goes down deeper, stays down longer, and comes up filthier.

The Bible recognizes the poison within man when it calls the heart "deceitful above things, and desperately wicked" (Jer. 7:9).

William Golding, author of the best-seller *Lord of the Flies,* claims that the novel's theme was an attempt to trace the defects of society back to the defects of human nature. The story relates the struggle of some boys—atomic war survivors—to reestablish civilization, and their resultant, tragic reversion to savagery. On a primitive island, pressured by basic human needs, the niceties of social and moral codes slowly crumble away from these happy children, revealing the dark, tangled jungle of human personality. From refinement begins the slide into cruelty, blood-lust, mutilation, even murder.

In the hunting and cornering of pigs the bestial nature of the boys expresses itself in their delight at thrusting their spears into the pigs, not once but repeatedly. The story ends in a dramatic hunt for a boy who has been their leader, against whom a rival faction turns, and who is saved by the arrival of a naval officer. The book ends with the officer heading off to war.

Termed a masterpiece of sheer narrative art, for the theme is conveyed entirely through the sensory and emotional impact of vivid storytelling, this book exposes the capacity for evil in all men.

The Imputation of Sin

That we are all sinners is a fact. The explanations of the relation of Adam's sin to the rest of the human race have resulted in various theories. Standard summaries of Christian doctrines such as *Outlines of Systematic Theology* by A. H. Strong (Judson Press, 1908, pp. 157-169) give the major views.

The Pelagian theory. Proponents of this theory maintain that Adam's sin affected only himself; that in no sense is his sin imputed to his descendants. Pelagius, a fifth-century monk, taught that Adam gave us a bad example, but not a bad nature. Every person is created as innocent as our first parent. God imputes to man, Pelagius said, only those acts which he personally and consciously performs. Thus man may be saved by keeping the Law perfectly.

The great weakness in the Pelagian theory lies in its contradiction of the biblical teaching that all have fallen short of God's glory in disposition as well as deed.

The Arminian theory. This theory, held by the early followers of Jacob Arminius, who lived in the 16th century, states that as a consequence of Adam's transgression, all men are naturally destitute of original righteousness. They are not accounted guilty of Adam's sin, however, because the grace of God extends to all.

But the Bible teaches that all men are not only unrighteous, but guilty as well, condemned to die and under the fearsome reality of God's wrath.

The Federal theory. In the 17th century, this theory was popular. It holds that Adam was God's sovereignly appointed representative of the entire human race. As a result of a covenant between God and Adam (the Latin term *foedus* means "covenant," hence "federal" theory) and Adam's failure to obey His Creator, God condemns all his descendants as sinners.

The Natural Headship theory. Augustine first elaborated this theory, and affirmed that, since the whole race at the time of Adam's sin existed in him as its head, we sinned in him. Adam's sin was imputed to us immediately because it was ours.

The various theories remind me of a tragic story I once heard. Fourteen mountain climbers in the Alps, roped to each other, fell to their death when their leader slipped. Though all theories of imputation have their critics, in some way Adam dragged the entire race down with disastrous results.

The Universality of Sin

An official in Washington, D.C., had a lighted globe on his desk, and on entering his office would often give it a twirl. When the globe stopped, he would point a finger at some spot without looking and exclaim, "There's trouble there!"

The Bible says there is no place or person in the world where sin isn't present. "All have sinned and come short of the glory of God" (Rom 3:23). The universal presence of sin is shown in several ways.

Direct statements of Scripture. "There is no man that sinneth not" (1 Kings 8:46). "All we like sheep have gone astray; we have turned every one to his own way" (Isa. 53:6; see also Ps. 14:2-3; 143:2; Ecc. 7:20; 1 John 1:8-10.)

The universal need of regeneration. In the Epistle to the Romans, before he describes the Gospel itself, Paul sets forth the universal need of the Gospel. All need salvation, he says, because all, without exception, are sinners: Gentiles, Jews, everyone (Rom. 1:18—3:20). He drives the truth home by a series of Old Testament quotes including, "There is none righteous, no, not one," and "there is none that seeketh after God" and "there is none that doeth good, no, not one" (Rom. 3:10-12).

If Paul's teaching on the universal sinfulness of mankind is untrue, the remainder of the Epistle is meaningless, for if no sin exists, what is the need for salvation?

The condemnation resting on all outside of Christ. Jesus plainly taught, "he that believeth not is condemned already . . . the wrath of God abideth on him" (John 3:18, 36).

The universal proclamation of the Gospel. Every creature in all the world stands in need of the Gospel (Matt. 28:19; Mark 16:15).

The common judgments of mankind. From experience, observation, and history, every man knows himself to be a sinner, and likewise knows that every other person has come short of moral perfection. Death is visited on everyone. And religions universally express a need to appease a deity from whom mankind everywhere senses alienation.

Though all persons have not sinned equally, yet all are equally sinners. An elderly lady and a teenage boy came to a bridgeless stream. The lady tried to jump the short span but landed with a splash in the middle of the water. The young man, boasting that jumping was a matter for youth, not age, took a long run, a big leap, and though he sailed farther than the elderly lady and almost made it, he too fell short and got just as soaked. Though some may surpass others in moral excellence, every member of the human race has fallen short of God's standard of perfection.

The biblical picture of fallen man is not pretty. In his natural estate, every member of Adam's posterity has a twisted, selfish, rebellious nature. The biggest delusion of all is to dream that, because we live in an advanced state of civilization, the lower passions of people are being diminished through advanced knowledge and material well-being. Man is as brutal as ever, even able to escalate his brutality to new heights of cruelty, because his capacity to maim is greater. Though proud human nature doesn't like to admit its depravity, this is the only realistic view which can account for our world's chaos.

A dear, old pillar of the church, after hearing the doctrine of original sin explained, exclaimed, "Well, if all of us are really as bad off as all that, then God help us!"

That's exactly what God did. God so loved the world that He sent His Son, Jesus Christ, to offset the penalty and power of sin.

7

What Does Sin Do to Us?

A billboard, widely displayed a few years ago, showed a tiger jumping into a car engine, with the slogan, "Put a tiger in your tank." Its TV counterpart depicted a tiger leaping into the engine of a car, the hood clicking shut, and the car purring away.

A Detroit advertising agency revealed how this harrowing commercial was filmed. First, they secured a tiger (a temperamental female named Patty), hired a film crew of 18 at $2,200 a day, removed the engine from the car, and placed the car over a shallow pit. They tried to entice the tiger to leap into the engine space. Her trainer held juicy chunks of raw beef down in the pit. But Patty refused to jump.

Thinking the feline might be camera shy, the crew hid. This time the tiger bounded on the car. But the hood slammed down on her paws. With a single, angry swipe, she ripped off the windshield wipers. The exhausted crew called it quits for the day.

Next day trying new tactics, the trainer ducked into the pit, holding live chickens. The chickens squawked. The cameras whirred. The tiger made a perfect leap into the open engine and down into the pit, emerging later in a flurry of feathers.

The ad graphically suggested that a tiger in the tank would add ferocity to your engine, making for pick-up, power, and speed. Have you ever thought that though no one really has a tiger in his tank, everyone has a tiger in his heart? Adam, having chosen his rebellious way, brought dire results, not only on himself, but also on all who followed. He willed to every member of the human race, not only a wicked example, but his own twisted nature with all its potentially explosive ferocity.

Theologians usually list three major effects of Adam's sin upon his posterity: depravity, guilt, and penalty.

Depravity

By depravity we mean not only the lack of original righteousness, but also the corruption of the moral nature, giving every person born into our world a bent toward evil.

This bias appears early in life. Sigmund Freud has shown that man is disorganized from his earliest days, never able to build up his ego and superego correctly. Even an infant, through its plaintive cry, deceives its mother into thinking it is hungry when all it wants is attention. The Bible says, "The wicked are estranged from the womb; they go astray as soon as they be born, speaking lies" (Ps. 58:3). David wrote, "I was shapen in iniquity; and in sin did my mother conceive me" (Ps. 51:5), meaning that humans possess a sinful nature from birth.

Nor does a sinful nature disappear in childhood. A child, when ordered not to touch the jam, not only disobeyed, but, on his mother's return, denied his disobedience, even though jam covered his little face. In another incident a girl said to her brother, "You're mean and selfish. You took the biggest apple and I wanted it." Children at games are quick to exclaim, "Me first!"

Adults are just as sinful. Have you ever watched people board a crowded bus at a busy hour? It's "shove thy neighbor" instead of "love thy neighbor." A bus driver in a sudden downpour of rain during the evening rush hour in New York City, unable to move passengers to the rear of the bus, pled, "Folks, these may be your neighbors you're making stand out there in the pouring rain." Then, with a broad grin he added, "Come to think of it, that may be why you're doing it!"

Five religious workers on a cross-country tour once carried

piles of literature with them in their small car, leaving barely enough room for two in the rear seat. Three had to sit up front, making it uncomfortable for the man in the middle. The only seat in this crowded car, with any degree of comfort, other than the driver's, was by the right front window. Though the others took turns sitting in the middle, one man invariably would rush from restaurant or meeting to ensure being seated in that desirable spot.

Some theologians describe man's nature as "totally depraved." Newsmen and police officers provide the evidence.

A few years ago the *New York Times* editorialized on the many acts of violence that appeared in its pages the previous day. The news on that single day included a story of 40 gang youths in Brooklyn battling with clubs, tire irons, and auto antennas; an account of a jeering mob in Uganda ripping a U.S. flag to shreds; the revelation of a plot of pro-Castro Communists to blow up the Statue of Liberty, the Washington Monument, and the Liberty Bell; the report of a bomb exploding at an entrance to Vatican City; and the revolting narrative of a pregnant woman in Manhattan stabbed 11 times as she fought off a youth trying to rape her in a hospital hallway. These were but a tip of the iceberg of all the frenzy which occurred that same day throughout the world. Such a chronicling of violence is a fever chart of a morally sick world.

The expression *total depravity* needs explanation. It does not mean that every sinner is devoid of conscience, nor that every person will be prone to every form of evil. Certain types exclude others. A man overproud of his honesty cannot be guilty of thievery. Nor does total depravity mean that every person will exert his maximum hatred toward his fellowmen and God, for he may be just indifferent to the needs of others and to the claims of God. Nor does it mean that he will be destitute of all commendable deeds, like helping a sick neighbor or contributing to the United Fund. Even convicts volunteer as guinea pigs for medical experiments; gangsters are often pictured as tender toward their animal pets. An alcoholic found lying on the sidewalk of Edinburgh, was clutching a doll he was carrying home to give to his sick little girl. Clearly, a Jekyll and Hyde mixture of good and evil exists in all of us.

But total depravity means, says Augustine, that "we are capable of every sin that we have seen our neighbor commit unless God's grace restrains us." Every sweet little baby sitting cutely in a high chair has the potential for doing the most dastardly deed imaginable.

A study of history seems to indicate that removal of social safeguards transforms men who have been respectable all their lives into lawless types. The young man who enlists in the army and the young lady who goes away to college find hometown and family barriers gone. They do things they would never have done in front of their parents. When natural disasters like hurricanes, tornados, floods, or earthquakes strike, otherwise seemingly honest citizens come in to pilfer the possessions of others until the National Guard moves in to protect property. In *The Devil's Share,* Denis De Rougemont argues that World War II gave decent people the occasion to act indecently. "The war was for us the great furlough, the great adjourning of our problems, the justification by public opinion of universal irresponsibility. We loved it, without realizing it, for one precise reason: it was the *state of exception* proclaimed on the entire earth and in all domains of public existence. . . . It had its most easily recognizable attributes: the overturning of the moral laws . . . the suspension of law; limitless expenditures; human sacrifices; disguises; processions; unleashing of collective passions" (Meridian Books, 1956, p. 77). Beneath the thin veneer of civilization lurks the deep-seated savagery of human depravity.

Total depravity also means that every person is totally devoid of that love and obedience to God which constitutes the all-inclusive demand of the Law; that every individual has a preference for self over God, which becomes active enmity when God's will comes into conflict with his own will; that all of his thoughts, words, and deeds are tinged with sin, thus without the full approval of God; that he is unable to perform spiritual good which merits salvation.

Finally, total depravity means that man's sinfulness extends to every part of his nature: mind, affections, and will.

Mind. That very power which differentiates us from the animals is tainted. The intellect is darkened (Eph. 4:18), and the natural mind does not receive the things of the Spirit (1 Cor. 2:14). Not only is man unable to find God by reason, but the carnal mind is "enmity against God" (Rom. 8:7; see also 2 Cor. 4:4; 1 Tim. 6:5; Titus 1:15.)

Rationalization, a term which reminds us of our God-given rational ability, in reality refers to the misuse of this power to excuse our misbehavior. To illustrate the human tendency to make excuses, one judge said he spent most of his time investigating collisions between vehicles, each on its own side of the road, each having sounded its horn, and each stationary.

Our intellectual depravity is reflected in this little verse:

> In a day of illusions
> And utter confusions
> Upon our delusions
> We base our conclusions.

Emotions. According to *Time* magazine, over 14,000 wars have been recorded in the last 5,000 years of history, or an average of 2.6 per year. In the early 1900s many believed this would be a "Christian century" with man abolishing war and crime. Now, toward the end of the century, with mankind grouped in armed camps with enough potential to blow the world into smithereens, many modern thinkers admit the old-fashioned, biblical view of the depravity of man.

No dangerous weapons exist, just dangerous people. The British periodical *Punch* says of the hydrogen bomb,

> "A pretty toy?" The devil shook his head;
> "I still prefer the human heart," he said.

Why are people unkind to each other, envious, nasty? What is it in man's make-up that will explain the brutality of concentration camps? Filling out a questionnaire surveying domestic relations, in a space for noting causes of friction in the home, one man wrote, "Me."

The reason for man's inhumanity to man is his depraved affections. Soon after the Fall, Cain envied, then murdered his brother.

Paul speaks of the unregenerate "living in malice and envy, hateful, and hating one another" (Titus 3:3).

Will. A small boy objected to his mother, "Don't say *must.* It makes me feel *won't* all over." In the same way, fallen man's will is in rebellion against God.

Our will is enslaved. To do good is unnatural; to do wrong is easy. We can drift into vice, but we cannot drift into virtue. A recent survey disclosed that 85% of public health nurses believe people should be convinced to stop smoking. But one-third were smokers themselves.

Enslaved by sinister forces, disoriented at the center, man is powerless to attain godliness on his own. God's initiative was essential for salvation. "God commendeth His love toward us, in that, while we were yet sinners, Christ died for us" (Rom. 5:8). Jesus said, "No man can come to Me, except the Father which hath sent Me draw him" (John 6:44). Man is spiritually dead in sins (Eph. 2:1).

In a centuries-long disagreement that will not be settled this side of heaven, Calvinists and Arminians differ over the condition of the human will. The Reformers—Luther and Calvin—held that man is dead in trespasses and sins, unable to respond to the call to believe unless God gives him life. John Wesley—an Arminian—modified the Calvinist teaching of total depravity, teaching that God cancelled the effects of original sin in the cross of Christ, thus giving to every person after Calvary the ability to respond to the call of the Gospel. In the Reformers' view man is dead; in Wesley's view he is sick. In American frontier evangelism, however, both revivalistic Calvinists and evangelical Arminians, coming from their two varying positions, arrived at basically the same spot—a Gospel of God's free grace that had to be accepted by morally responsible men.

Guilt

Guilty means "worthy of punishment," or an obligation to render satisfaction to God's justice for self-determined violation of the Law. God's holiness reacts against sin. Guilt is the sinner's relation to that holiness, his deserved expectancy of penalty.

Objective guilt. Guilt is the objective result of sin whereas depravity is subjective pollution. Every sin, because it offends God, must be expiated by either punishment or atonement (Heb. 9:22).

Objective guilt, called a "debt to God" (Matt. 6:12), is not to be confused with subjective guilt, which is a relation to one's conscience. Subjective guilt may be marked by decreasing sensitivity or by increasing neuroticism, while objective guilt remains constant till forgiveness is secured, at which time subjective guilt should disappear.

Degrees of guilt. Different degrees of guilt are attached to different kinds of sin. For example, the person who commits adultery in his mind is not as guilty as the one who commits it in actuality.

Sins of ignorance bring less blameworthiness than sins of knowledge. Guilt is measured by the degree of light men possess, or by opportunities of knowledge enjoyed, or by talents with which endowed. The heathen are guilty, but those who hear the Gospel bear greater culpability. The servant who knows the Lord's will, but does not do it will be beaten with many stripes, whereas the servant who does not know it will be beaten with few stripes (Luke 12:47-48). Jesus said, "It shall be more tolerable for the land of Sodom and Gomorrah in the day of judgment" than for those cities which heard Him give a message in person (Matt. 10:15; see also Rom. 2:12).

Sins of infirmity, committed in haste or weakness, will bring some palliation of penalty. But those done in full awareness will bring far greater guilt. The Psalmist prayed to be kept from "presumptuous sins" (Ps. 19:13).

The sin of temporary opposition to the Holy Spirit is forgivable, but the sin of final hardheartedness is unforgivable (Matt. 12:31-32). A heart radically set against God becomes so self-hardening and self-depraving that it ceases to be receptive to divine influence, and thus is permanently beyond help.

Penalty

"Penalty" means the pain or loss inflicted on the sinner by the

Lawgiver in vindication of justice which has been outraged by the violation of the Law. The purpose of the penalty is not the reformation of the offender, not deterrence to observers. The primary purpose is the vindication of the holy character of the divine Lawgiver.

The one word in Scripture which designates the total penalty of sin is *death*. The key concept in death is separation. Physical death is the separation of body and soul. Spiritual death is the separation of the soul from God. Eternal death is the culmination and completion of spiritual death, resulting in final and permanent separation of the sinner from the presence of a holy God.

Because of the Fall, death is a terrible enemy. He cares not for our plans. A lady may start a letter she will never sign. A man may begin a journey he will never complete. A youth may enroll in a college program he will never finish. Though life expectancy has doubled from the 35-year span of 1776, everyone reading this paragraph will someday die (unless Christ returns first), as a consequence of Adam's sin.

A few years before World War II, a German pastor, noting hopeless despair on the faces of young men who couldn't find work, founded the "University of the Unemployed." He hoped their terrible feeling of worthlessness could be overcome by transforming these nonworking young men into students. Soon 500 aspiring young men were meeting every morning in the rooms of the church for classes in English, French, mathematics, agriculture, music, stenography, Esperanto, jujitsu, architecture, and other subjects. The teachers also came from the ranks of the unemployed.

The high hour of the week was the philosophy period, in which the pastor preached the Gospel for 20 minutes, then asked for discussion. Because of the varied composition of the group, young Communists, storm troopers in brown uniforms, hard hats, socialists, fanatics, cynics, atheists, sectarians, idealists, and some believers, the room often became a raging battlefield, which had to be calmed by the pastor. Without exception, the Gospel was swept out of the way in the first few minutes of discussion. Of course, they expected the pastor to talk like this, but who could take such antiquated teaching seriously? They were quick to set forth their ideologies, the teachings of Lenin, the doctrines of Hitler, the economics of Marx. The poor pastor wondered how he could make any impact with his simple Gospel against all these zealously espoused, ready-made solutions for world problems. Things might have continued, had it not been for the episode of the rolls.

On a two-day retreat sponsored by the pastor, as the 150 hikers sat in cozy weariness drying their rain-drenched clothes around a fireplace, the local baker appeared to ask if any wanted rolls in the morning. His price was four rolls for 10 pfennigs, a lot of money for an unemployed person. For that amount one could have three cigarettes, and besides, rye bread would be available for breakfast. About 50 youths decided to order rolls. The other 100 chose to go without. The atmosphere relaxed enough for the pastor to conduct an evening meditation. That night, Communist slept peacefully next to storm trooper, and idealist beside cynic.

But next morning the pastor was awakened by enraged shouting and angry scuffling. A battle had disrupted the peace of the previous evening. The trouble had begun when the baker arrived with rolls for the 50 who had ordered them. The rolls smelled so delicious that those who hadn't ordered the night before rushed at the baker and tore the rolls from his hands. Many who had ordered were empty-handed. That is when fighting had broken out.

With difficulty the pastor gained attention. Then he demanded all the rolls surrendered to him. Soon he had a mountain of rolls before him, and asked who really wanted rolls. He doled them out one to a person. Then he asked the baker if he could provide 400 more in half an hour. He could.

How peaceful the breakfast. The day dawned beautifully. The pastor had scheduled morning devotions under an old tree. He began, "Friends, we all agree on one thing. The world must change. For several months now in every philosophy hour I've been hearing how each of you has a ready-made political or economic program to save the world. But now I'm disappointed that you who thought you could save the world with your ideologies couldn't even divide 200 rolls peaceably. What good are your philosophies if they fail so miserably in little things?"

The young men sat silent, stunned. The pastor continued, "Why did it happen? Because everyone thought only of himself. Your wicked hearts played a trick on you and spoiled everything. You have always acted as if the Bible were a dull, outdated book. Now I tell you that the Bible is right. It says the human heart is selfish and sinful and deceitful. And here in the Bible it tells how our hearts can become new. Here we learn of one sent by God, who through His blood and Spirit, can transform us and make us new. That one is Jesus Christ." As the birds sang and a summer breeze stirred the old tree under which they were gathered, the pastor knew that something of divine glory had touched the hearts of these young men (*Decision* magazine, October 1964, p. 7).

Because of the Fall, man is alienated from God, estranged from and at enmity with his brother, and deeply divided in his inmost self. Out of communion with God—for no longer did God come walking in the cool of the day to fellowship with Adam—man became a sinful, selfish creature in need of transformation and beyond the power of self-cures.

But transformation is possible. Through the redemptive work of Jesus Christ the Saviour, man's governing disposition can be changed, so that he will not be selfish, but sacrificial; not greedy, but giving. When crooked Zaccheus let Christ into his life, he who had become rich through fraud found his heart so changed that he gave away half of his wealth, besides repaying fourfold everyone he had cheated. When the Philippian jailor let Christ into his heart, he who had earlier that evening roughly thrust Paul and Silas into the inner dungeon and fastened their feet in stocks, served them dinner in his own home and washed their bruised backs as well.

The tiger in man's heart can be overcome. The Lion of the tribe of Judah, who came to earth as the Lamb of God, can conquer and control our fallen nature.

8

Do You Live on the Highest Level?

After the shootings and shellings of the 1976 civil strife in Beirut, Lebanon, a man noticed the top story of a three-level bombed-out building. All that remained was a shell. People, however, were living on the first and second floors.

That building is a picture of man. In his unregenerate condition he lives only on his first two levels. Though his top story is, by nature, empty, it has the capacity for occupancy. So we ask, "Is your upper story occupied? Do you live on the highest level?"

For the sake of illustration, let us imagine ourselves a building, consisting of three stories.

The First Story Is Our Body
The philosophy of Idealism holds that material substance, apart from our idea of it, does not exist. Only thinking substance, soul or spirit exist. The body is nothing but the extension of an idea.

The Bible, however, does not deny or minimize man's body. It teaches that God created the body and that God the Son, came to redeem sinful men by assuming a human body.

This difference between Greek idealistic philosophy and biblical faith was sharply underscored when the Apostle Paul appealed to Christian believers to present their *bodies* as living sacrifices to

God (Rom. 12:1-2). That sort of appeal made no sense to a Greek who demeaned the body.

> Assigned an essay on anatomy, one youngster wrote, Your head is kind of round and hard and your brains is in it and your hair is on it. Your face is the front of your head where you eat and make faces. Your neck is what keeps your head out of your collar. It's hard to keep clean. Your stummick is something that if you don't eat often enough, it hurts and spinach don't help none. Your spine is a long bone in your back that keeps you from folding up. Your back is always behind you no matter how quick you turn around. Your arms you got to pitch with and so you can reach the butter. Your fingers stick out of your hands. Your legs get you to first base. Your feet are what you run on, and your toes are what always get stubbed. And that's all there is on you 'cept what's inside, and I ain't seen that.

He was right about more on the inside, not only internal organs, but the inner, immaterial man—the soul. In terms of our building illustration—man has more than one story. He is more than a body.

Man Is Body Plus

Some modern philosophers hold that man is only body, and that mind, soul, or spirit cannot exist as an independent entity. The mind, they maintain, is simply the by-product of bodily or chemical processes, and personality is nothing more than the organization of brain waves. At death the entire man dissolves into dust. One psychology professor told his students to hang their souls on the doorknob when they entered his class.

In the Marxist view, man is essentially matter; thinking is simply the product of his economic conditioning. Since in this system, evil is reduced to private ownership of property, redemption is found in the transfer of private property to the control of the state.

For half a century Communism has had an opportunity to demonstrate the virtues of a classless society. But it exhibits absolute dictatorship and operates a monstrous system of slave labor. When man bears the price tag of matter only, human life is dirt cheap. Bestial cruelty and inhumanity logically follow. No wonder our century has witnessed the horrors of concentration camps. Why not regard man as essentially worthless if, after all, he is simply a soulless organism brought into existence by the same forces that produce rust on a tin roof and fungus on a rock?

But man is more than body. Two men were looking into a glass case, containing an exhibit of all the chemical elements in the human body. One remarked, "So, that's all I am." The other responded, "No, sir, there's something in you that can't be put in a glass case."

The Bible says that the Lord God formed man's body from the dust of the earth, breathed into his nostrils the breath of life, making man a living soul and creating him in His own image (Gen. 2:7; 1:27). Man is not the freak product of blind cosmic force, some accidental grouping of atoms, but the result of God's deliberate plan, body plus soul. Christ told His disciples not to fear the person who could kill only body, but rather to fear the one who could destroy both soul and body in hell (Matt. 10:28).

In Harriet Beecher Stowe's *Uncle Tom's Cabin,* poor Uncle Tom, severely thrashed and asked by his cruel master, "How would you like to be tied to a tree and have a slow fire lit up around you?" replied that after his master has killed his body there wasn't any more he could do. He was right. There is a part of us no fire can burn, no whip can touch, no noose can hang.

Christ told the dying thief that he would be with Him in Paradise, which means that the thief was more than the body that was later removed from the cross (Luke 23:43). Paul also taught that man was body plus, for to be absent from the body means to be present with the Lord, and departing this body means to be "with Christ" (2 Cor. 5:8; Phil. 1:23).

Belief in the existence of the soul is no longer widely dismissed. An Arizona gold miner disappeared in 1949 at the age of 71 while out on a prospecting trip. A bachelor, with no close relatives or friends, little was known about him. Eighteen years later his money and a handwritten will were found in a vault of a bank that was about to be razed. The will said that aside from funeral expenses and $100 for a "preacher of the Gospel to say farewell at my grave," the rest of the money should go for research or some other scientific proof of "a soul of a human body which leaves at death." The old miner added, "I think there can be a photograph of a soul leaving the human at death."

About 140 groups and individuals laid claim to the fortune, which rose, through added bank interest, from its original worth of $175,000 to nearly $300,000. It was finally awarded to the American Society for Psychiatrical Research, Inc., of New York. The society was founded in 1906 by William James and once counted among its membership Sigmund Freud and Margaret Mead. Its major purpose is to investigate parapsychological events.

Experience supports the commonsense view that we have a real physical body and a real immaterial soul, which function together in this life as an interacting unity. A Christian lawyer witnessing to a stranger, asked if all were well with his soul. The young stranger laughed, "There's no such thing as a soul. I just got out of college. No one believes that superstition anymore. I don't believe in anything I can't see. Show me your soul."

Seeming to change the subject, the lawyer said, "You must have finished pretty high in your class. You have a sharp mind." When the young man admitted that he had above average intelligence, the lawyer asked him to show his intellect, adding, "I don't believe in anything I can't see!"

Then the lawyer, forcing the youth to acknowledge that he had not only intellect, but ambition, memory, and a host of other qualities that he could not show, concluded by pointing out that all these unseen properties inhere in a unifying entity called the soul.

Have you ever considered that you really don't see a person, you see only the body in which he lives? The real person is somewhere within that body, somewhere in front of his back, and in back of his front. Woodrow Wilson's favorite limerick went like this:

> I know I'm ugly I are,
> I know my face ain't no star,

But I don't mind it
Cause I'm behind it;
It's the fellow in front who gets the jar.

Two-Storied or Three-Storied?

Our illustration of man as a building, with the body as the first story, raises the question of whether man has two stories or three? Is man dichotomous (two-part) or trichotomous (three-part)? Is man a body and soul-spirit (two)? Or is he body, soul, and spirit (three)?

Those who hold that man in a trichotomy put strong emphasis on two texts: 1 Thessalonians 5:23 and Hebrews 4:12. But when Paul wrote, "I pray God your whole *spirit* and *soul* and *body* be preserved blameless unto the coming of our Lord Jesus Christ," he wasn't distinguishing the parts of man, but simply heaping word upon word to emphasize completeness of preservation. Christ did the same thing when He commanded love to God "with all thy heart, and with all thy soul, and with all thy mind, and with all thy strength" (Mark 12:30). He was piling up word upon word to stress the completion of devotion which should be ours, not teaching that man has four parts.

Similarly, when the writer of Hebrews stated that the word of God, sharper than any two-edged sword, could divide asunder soul and spirit, he didn't mean it could make two separate entities out of man's immaterial part, any more than by its ability to divide asunder joints and marrow could it make two separate entities out of man's material part, the body.

Those who maintain that man is dichotomous, point out that the term *soul* and *spirit* are used interchangeably. For example, in Mary's "Magnificat," her *soul* magnifies the Lord, and her *spirit* rejoices in God her Saviour (Luke 1:46-47). Death is represented as giving up the *soul* and giving up the *spirit* (Gen. 35:18; Acts 7:59). The dead are sometimes called *souls,* and often *spirits* (Rev. 6:9; 1 Peter 3:19). The Bible formula for man is sometimes body and *soul,* and in other cases body and *spirit* (Matt. 10:28; 1 Cor. 5:5).

This dual representation harmonizes with man's self-consciousness of a material and an immaterial part, but without distinction between soul and spirit. In all of its activity the soul-spirit remains together as one. For example, at death when the body is buried, the soul-spirit leaves for its eternal destination as one entity, not with the soul heading off in one direction, and the spirit in another.

Even though the immaterial part of man is one entity (soul-spirit), perhaps soul and spirit have different functions within the whole. Could we say that the soul is the self-conscious thinking faculty, whereas the spirit is the capacity for communion with God? If we accept this differentiation our illustration of a building must represent man as a modified dichotomy. It must show man with "two main floors": body and soul-spirit. But the second story must be divided by a broken line to indicate separate functions within the soul-spirit, virtually making man a three-story creature.

The Second Story Is the Soul

Following our illustration, we may call the second story the "soul." This part of us, made in God's image, has among other qualities the ability to reason, communicate, invent, enjoy beauty, and appreciate humor. The Bible suggests this diversity when some Hebrew words meaning "heart," "soul," or even "spirit," are sometimes translated *mind* (Isa. 65:17). A little girl who was asked what her soul was replied, "Sir, my soul is my Think." She wasn't far from the truth.

The Upper Story Is the Spirit

Materialists say "Man is what he eats." Educators claim, "man is what he reads." Jesus, however, said that man cannot live by bread (or books) alone, but by every word that proceeds from the mouth of God (Matt. 4:4). Man was created by God for fellowship with Himself.

At the beginning, when God and man walked together in the cool of the day, man's spirit, the God-conscious part, was in control of the whole man. "At the Fall," says J. Stafford Wright, "the spirit of man dropped out of communion with God, and so the whole man fell into ruin. So long as the spirit is cut off from God and His new life, the whole man is in a state of death. Thus the possession of eternal life depends upon the rebirth of the human spirit by the incoming of the Holy Spirit of life.

"Meanwhile there still remains the original central control-house in man, namely the human spirit, which is of very little use until it has been born again. . . . This spirit has no power of regenerating itself; it is not a divine spark that can be fanned into a flame; and until a man has been born again by the Spirit of God, he is 'natural' . . . and only becomes 'spiritual' . . . at the new birth" (*Man in the Process of Time,* Eerdmans, 1956, pp. 152-153).

Man's Upper Story Is Empty

Because man's upper story (spirit) at birth does not have the life of God, man does not have control over the lower stories (mind and body). This is why with all the scientific advances of recent years our world finds itself in its present mess. Our moral brakes do not match our mental horsepower. We have the means to master the earth but cannot control ourselves. Someone has said, "We have learned to fly in the air like birds, to swim under water like fish, but we haven't learned how to walk on the earth like men." A British paper summed it up, "Man has conquered the air, only to be compelled to burrow under the ground."

Through the centuries our knowledge has so often been mis-used. We learned to make airplanes, then turned them into bombers. We researched atomic energy, then invented the atom bomb. We discovered movies and TV, then degraded them with violence and sex.

Education (a product of our second story) cannot control human nature. An American sailor met an old friend on a South Sea island who had returned to his practice of cannibalism after graduation from an American university. "But didn't your college training affect your cannibalism in any way?" asked the surprised American sailor. "Sure did," explained the national, "now in the cannibal feasts I eat with knife and fork."

Education enables us to kill with more refinement. A few

hundred years ago we could fell enemies one at a time by means of bow and arrow, sword, or hammer, but today thanks to our sophistication we can destroy thousands with a single bomb.

When the controversial supersonic Concorde was in its trial transatlantic flights in 1976, a cartoon showed a bandaged patient in a London hospital remarking to his roommate, "You have to hand it to the Concorde—I got mugged in New York and in London the same day."

When the late Mayor Curley of Boston was serving time in federal prison, he learned that practically every college in the country was represented among the inmates, including Harvard, Yale, Columbia, and West Point. One day in the prison library a kindly old man asked Curley if he remembered him. It turned out that Curley had addressed the graduating class of the Massachusetts Institute of Technology when this man received his degree.

As Stuart Barton Babbage put it, "If you want a bomb, the chemistry department will teach you how to make it; if you want a cathedral, the department of architecture will teach you how to build it; if you want a healthy body, the department of physiology and medicine will teach you how to tend it. But when you ask whether and why you should want bombs or cathedrals or healthy bodies, the university is dumb and impotent" (*Christianity Today,* April 12, 1974, p. 57). Education can give guidance on all subsidiary, second-floor matters, but no direction in the top area of life, for man's upper story is empty.

On Which Story Do Most People Live?

On what level do people spend most of their time and energy: body, mind, or spirit?

Don't most people live on the first floor? At a state fair, the prize exhibit was a live python from India, 40 feet long, and weighing 300 pounds. When a visitor complained because only a glass partition separated the monster from the public, the attendant replied, "Mister, you have nothing to fear. See how it's contentedly curled up. I keep its stomach full of hamburger, and the thermostat set to keep it sleeping all the time it's not eating. It's as harmless as a puppy!" Are people significantly different from that python? For many, the great American dream is to satisfy our creature comforts.

Granted, we do have physical needs that require attention. But a casual glance at magazine advertisements and TV commercials reveals that far too much space is assigned our first story. Life seems to consist of foods, cosmetics, clothes, health, beauty, sex, and sports.

A taxi driver complained to his fare, "My dentist told me not to smoke or drink, or have soda or chew gum. What else is there to live for?" For most people, nothing. Motel signs often read, "Food—Pool—Cocktails." That is the sum of a lower-story appeal.

Alexander Pope in his *Essay on Man* writes of man's dilemma,

> In doubt to deem himself a god, or beast;
> In doubt his mind or body to prefer.

Though the *Reader's Digest* has run a series of articles on the various body organs, such as "I Am Joe's Heart," it seems unlikely it will ever do one on "I Am Joe's Soul."

Some people do prefer the mind. There is life on the second story. Interests may vary: literature, history, political science, biology, chemistry, philosophy, poetry, sculpture, music, painting. A man who wanted to know how his favorite team was doing in the baseball game walked over to a table in the restaurant where a customer was listening intently to a small transistor radio. "What's the score?" he asked. The radio listener removed his earplug, and wistfully smiled, "Beethoven's Ninth!"

Comparatively few, however, live on the third level, the spiritual. Many who appreciate cultural pursuits are void of moral control. A sadistic Nazi doctor at the Auschwitz concentration camp, known as the "Angel of Death" since he was in charge of selections for the gas chambers, used to ride around the vast camp on his bicycle, whistling tunes by Mozart.

How few walk with the Lord day by day, the windows of their spirit open to His presence. The cry of the Roman populace was "bread and circus," something to fill the body and something to amuse the mind, but no request for anything to satisfy the spirit.

Whom do Americans reward most highly for the services they

render? According to one survey, physicians head the list, with dentists third—men who care for the needs of the first-story body. Sixth and seventh are scientists and educators, who deal in the area of the second-story mind. The ministry, which majors in the upper-story spirit, ranks eighth.

Who is more popular on a college campus: the football coach, the Latin professor, or the chaplain? Which gets the biggest crowd: the football game, the debate, or the Bible study? A university is an institution with room for 200 in its chapel, 2,000 in its classrooms, and 20,000 in its stadium.

Who gives more concern to most parents: a child who is sick, a child not progressing well at school, or a child with little interest in spiritual matters?

A Sunday newspaper carried the following listing in its radio schedule: "1 P.M. 'Back to God (If no World Series game)."

Would not many people have to admit that very little time, if any, has been given during the last month to matters of the spirit? That, in fact, their upper story is empty? Doesn't this explain why, despite our materialistic, pleasure-loving, jet-set society, most Americans experience an anxious emptiness deep within?

An Occupied Upper Story

How can your upper story be occupied? First, recognize that naturally this story is empty. Man is born out of fellowship with God, void of divine righteousness, minus the life of God. By nature he cares little for the things of God, seldom darkens the door of a church, and rarely gives God any more than a fleeting thought. The natural man does not welcome the things of the Spirit.

Then, realize that the redemptive work of Christ makes possible God's presence in your upper story. Adam's sin was the reason God no longer had fellowship with man. Christ came to pay the penalty for sin, making possible man's reconciliation with God. Through Calvary's cross the barrier has been removed so that God can justify the sinner and renew fellowship with him.

Finally, invite the Lord Jesus Christ into your life. He says, "Behold, I stand at the door and knock: if any man hear My voice, and open the door, I will come in to him, and will sup with him, and he with Me" (Rev. 3:20).

At your invitation He will come in to occupy your upper story and control your life: spirit, mind and body.

9

Is There Life after Death?

Dr. Elisabeth Kubler-Ross, Swiss-born Illinois psychiatrist, is known internationally for spelling out the five emotional stages experienced by terminally ill patients. After years of counseling the dying, she has come to the conviction that life continues after death. She is impressed by the evidence of out-of-body consciousness, that is, the apparent ability of people who have exhibited no breathing, no heartbeat, or no brain-wave activity, to later describe events that took place around them. According to Dr. Kubler-Ross, if a woman, declared dead in a hospital, can later tell you exactly how many people walked into the room and worked on her, this cannot be hallucination.

Another physician, Dr. Raymond A. Moody, Jr., who holds a doctorate in philosophy as well as in medicine, has published a book, relating interviews with 50 people who had near-death experiences. Often these folks heard themselves pronounced dead by doctors, or had a great sense of peace, or heard pleasant music, or related a sensation of moving out of their bodies and floating toward the ceiling from which they looked down on themselves as doctors worked over their bodies on the operating table. Dr. Moody believes that many of these near-death experiences cannot be readily explained away as delusions induced by pain-killing drugs. He titled his book, *Life after Life* (Mockingbird Books, Inc., Covington, Georgia, 30209).

Is there life beyond the grave? Twenty centuries ago Caesar stood in the Roman Senate and said, "If there be anything beyond death, I do not know." In our century Bertrand Russell, the British philosopher, wrote, "I believe that when I die, I shall rot, and nothing of my ego will survive."

When Spain thought herself the westward boundary of the world, she stamped on her coins the Pillar of Hercules with this inscription, *Ne Plus Ultra,* meaning "No More Beyond." When we are confronted by the remains in the casket, the listless eye, the motionless hand, the silent voice, everything on the surface seems to carry this message, "Nothing on the other side." But when Columbus discovered a new world beyond, Spain erased the "no," leaving "more beyond." Do we have enough information to accept the existence of life beyond? The age-old question is asked in the Book of Job, "If a man die, shall he live again?" (14:14)

Almost All Cultures Hold Some Belief in a Future Existence

The late First Lady Eleanor Roosevelt once wrote in her syndicated column, "Almost every person with whom I have ever talked in my world travels has believed in life after death." Tennyson wrote, "If there is no immortality, I shall hurl myself into the sea." Bismarck, a little more restrained, said, "Without the hope of an afterlife, this life is not even worth the effort of getting dressed in the morning." Freud described the belief that death is the door to a better life as "the oldest, strongest, and most insistent wish of mankind."

The Pyramids of Egypt would be nearly as perfect today as when built 5,000 years ago, were it not for attacking marauders and souvenir-seeking tourists. The Egyptians, more than any other ancient people, entombed with their dead a vast array of material objects for the journey though another world. In the tomb were stocked items such as furniture, food, weapons, extra clothing, gems, perfumes, make-up kits, and mirrors.

As private fortunes increased, tomb structures and furnishings multiplied. The largest pyramid, located outside Cairo, is composed of 2,300,000 limestone blocks, each weighing two-and-a-half tons, measuring 755 feet, 6 inches on each side of the base. Despite its great size, maximum deviation from perfect symmetry today is less than one inch. This engineering marvel, one of the Seven Wonders of the World, eloquently testifies that when mankind was still in its cradle, the race possessed a firm belief in immortality.

Lew Wallace, author of *Ben Hur,* once said, "The monuments of the nations are all protests against nothingness after death; so are statues and inscriptions; so is history."

On exhibition at Wheaton College, Illinois, is the skeleton of a small child discovered in 1953 by members of the college's Archaeology Department digging at Dothan, 60 miles north of Jerusalem. The infant died about 4,000 years ago around the age of two.

Because the bones were so brittle, the archaeologists used shellac to keep them from crumbling. It took two days of painstaking work to unearth them. Also uncovered close by were three jugs and a bowl. These utensils were buried with the baby because the Canaanites believed in immortality.

Plato, an ancient Greek philosopher, gave several arguments for the immortality of the soul in his dialogue, *Phaedo,* among them the doctrine of recollection. An uneducated slave-boy was asked to ascertain the area of a square, double the size of a given square. Through questioning he was led to supply the correct answer: the square on the diagonal of the original square. Since the lad didn't learn it, Plato argued that he must have recollected it from a previous existence. Therefore, Plato concluded, the soul survives death.

In certain past cultures a servant was often buried alive with his master, or a wife with her husband, because it was believed the servant or wife could be of service to the deceased in the world to come.

Though the survival of the soul after death seems to have been a common concept in all ages and cultures, various views of immortality are held.

One belief is that we live on only in the grateful memory of posterity. According to this view, people might live on in their children or through their creative works. That was apparently the thought of the friend who tried to console a terminally ill politician with talk about the immortality of influence.

Another view says that the soul returns to its original source (some sort of spirit of God) at death. According to this pantheistic theory, the individual does not himself survive but joins "the whole" from which it was temporarily separated. Personality does not persist.

Still another theory is that the soul has always existed, and will continue to do so forever. By definition the soul is eternal, going through an endless series of existences, occupying a different body during each incarnation. A form of this doctrine of transmigration of the soul was broadly held in the ancient world.

The biblical view holds that the soul is immortal, but not eternal. To be eternal the soul would have to be without beginning, as well as without end. But the soul did not always exist. The soul had a beginning sometime between conception and birth. It is uniquely joined to one human body, but can exist separately from that body, surviving as a person after death. The Christian belief also affirms the resurrection of that body (discussed in the next chapter) to join the same soul prior to judgment. Thus, the biblical doctrine holds to the unity and interdependence of body and soul. Man is neither soul only, or body only, or a soul using a body, but *soul and body*.

The idea of life after death seems inseparably woven into the very fabric of man's nature, an impression existing universally, from which he cannot permanently free himself—despite the fact that the earth is one vast cemetery. Man's wish for immortality suggests his dread of disappearance into mere nothingness. Subconsciously he senses the need to be linked to the permanent and resists the suggestion of utter annihilation.

A newspaper picture a few years ago showed a top Russian leader standing by the grave of his wife who had just died in midlife. A tear could be detected on his cheek as he was in the act of throwing a fir sprig into the open grave. An American Russian Christian expressed surprise. "Branch-tossing is a custom of

Russian believers to express their hope of life beyond the grave," he said. "And here is the head of an avowed atheistic state who just cannot get away from this truth!"

Someone said, "We do not believe in immortality because we have proved it, but we forever try to prove it because we believe it."

A Gallup Poll in 1976 showed 69% of American people believe in life after death, a figure that has remained constant since 1948.

Is it because the human heart so expects life after death that, in speaking of the many mansions in His Father's house, Jesus said, "If it were not so, I would have told you"? (John 14:2)

Life Here Is Incomplete and Imperfect

In a Spanish cathedral hang the paintings of a fine artist known only as El Greco. Some of his apostles and saints are just bare, unfinished sketches, mere outlines of a hand or face. Death's cold grip overtook El Greco before he could finish his work. We all sense the problem. Life is too short to complete all the tasks we aim to do. Human nature is simply inexplicable on the basis of a few short years on earth. We feel that more than 70 or 80 years are needed to make life meaningful. There has to be a nobler and more enduring state of existence. One man quipped, "I'm so far behind in the things I'm supposed to do. There's got to be another life so I can catch up."

Intellectually. The scale of man's potential is too large for his present limited life. Man has a thirst for knowledge. What vast fields are available and ever expanding! Some wit defined a specialist as someone who knows more and more about less and less until he knows everything about nothing. When a doctor who had been a throat, nose, and ear man decided to specialize in the nose, someone asked, "Which nostril?"

Robert Oppenheimer once said, "We know too much for one man to know much." There has to be life after death to give time and opportunity for man to learn more, satisfy his mind, and complete his inadequate information. A poet wrote, referring to Sir Isaac Newton's statement that in this life he seemed able to gather only little pebbles of knowledge,

> "I know not how my work may seem to others—"
> So wrote our mightiest mind—"but to myself
> I seem a child that wandering all day long
> Upon the seashore gathers here a shell,
> And there a pebble, colored by the wave,
> While the great ocean of truth, from sky to sky,
> Stretches before him, boundless, unexplored."
>
> Alfred Noyes in *Watchers of the Sky*

The capacity of the mind seems boundless, able to travel off into space, span the universe, reach back in time, and to some extent take in thought of God, eternity, and infinity. Is such a mind confined to 80 years? Robert Browning wrote (*Pauline, Work 1*),

> I cannot chain my soul; it will not rest
> In its clay prison, this most narrow sphere.
> It has strange powers, and feelings, and desires,
> Which I cannot account for nor explain,
> But which I stifle not, being bound to trust
> All feeling equally, to hear all sides.
> Yet I cannot indulge them, and they live,
> Referring to some state of life unknown.

A late-life picture of Sir Winston Churchill caught him painting on a canvas, with all the vitality he gave the task of defeating Hitler. He sits by the Mediterranean, a tightly bitten cigar in his mouth, brush splashing away, a portrait of a man having a whale of a time. In his memoirs he confessed, "When I get to painting, I envy Methuselah."

So often human aspirations go unfulfilled. One man, who accomplished a great deal in life, lamented on his 80th birthday, "How small a part of my lifework have I been able to do. Life at its fullest is only a fragment." Many people dream of seeing the world but never set foot on foreign soil.

Lawrence B. Saint, an artist in stained glass, was able to finish 15 windows with biblical themes in the lovely National Episcopal Cathedral in Washington, D.C. Life, however, didn't give him the opportunity to realize his hope of painting the entire Bible in stained glass. May not the hereafter provide that opportunity? A poet wrote:

> My Lord, I do not understand;
> Thou giv'st me threescore years and ten,
> To make and mold my life, and then,
> Dear Lord, to make one perfect tree,
> A thousand years are not for Thee
> Too many years for Thy wise hand
> To make this redwood tree—
> And threescore years and ten are given to men!
> Behold this pebble at my feet;
> Round, smooth and white—a perfect stone;
> Ten thousand times ten thousand years have flown
> Since this one was begun!
> And I have threescore years and ten—
> A thousand years to make a tree,
> A million years to make a stone,
> And then, despite our prayers and tears,
> A span of threescore years and ten
> Is given to men?
> Let be! My body is the seed;
> For me is made Eternity.
>
> Author unknown

As someone aptly put it, "This life is not the book—it is only the first chapter of the book."

Morally. It takes time to build the character of a godly person. Would God take the major part of someone's lifetime progressively sanctifying him in the image of His Son, and then when He had almost finished His work, dash him to pieces or annihilate him? What a waste! What would we think of a sculptor who, after three laborious decades on a block of marble, had chiseled a statue approaching faultless proportion and perfect facial expression, only to smash the statue to pieces and toss the bits into the ash can?

William James of Harvard once said that his interest in personal immortality grew much stronger as he grew older "because I am just getting fit to live."

The radical imperfection of human existence calls for a day to come when the wrongs of this life are righted. We are told not to fret because of evildoers, for they will be cut down like the grass (Ps. 37:1-2). But when? How can justice be administered and rewards doled out, unless there is a day of reckoning ahead?

Were Moses and Pharaoh on the same moral level? Elijah and Jezebel? John the Baptist and Herodias? Peter and Judas? The Pharisees and Stephen? The martyrs and their persecutors? Must truth be forever on the scaffold and wrong forever on the throne? If right is to triumph, there must be immortality.

A widow who had fought frequently and furiously with her husband had this inscription placed on his tombstone, "Rest in peace—till we meet again." On a more positive level, the incompleteness of human love seems to suggest a future life for fulfillment and reunion. Death breaks up long-time marriages and dissolves friendships. Resumption of human fellowship requires a life beyond. Charles Kingsley, English clergyman and novelist, selected for his tombstone three Latin words, which translated mean, "We have loved, we do love, we shall love." Without a hereafter, love here will be lost.

Human nature finds its greatest impetus under the influence of immortality. Belief in a future life gives comfort in tragedy as well as motivation to moral living. A belief in two worlds makes us better in this one. Someone put it, "He sins against this life who slights the next." If only this world exists, life becomes a ghastly nightmare and not worth living. Or as the Apostle Paul put it, "If in this life only we have hope in Christ, we are of all men most miserable" (1 Cor. 15:19).

The Bible Teaches Life beyond Death

Science, philosophy, mysticism, and religion are unable to tell us for sure that there is life beyond death. The only book to which we can turn is the Bible.

Neither so-called communication with the dead via mediums, nor supposed dreams of previous existence, nor reported visions which dying people seem to have of loved ones in heaven, are conclusive proof of life beyond.

Dr. Elisabeth Kubler-Ross gives as some of her reasons for believing in life after death:

(1) the peaceful expressions that come over most patients a minute or so after death, even those who struggled terribly with death;

(2) the conversations that people on their deathbeds have with departed loved ones;

(3) the testimony of folks revived through medical intervention after "clinical" death, who tell of floating out of the body, of beholding what is happening to the corpse, of seeing when they had been blind, and of being whole when they had previously been without a limb.

The well-known Christian writer, Joseph Bayly, however, cautions against eagerly grabbing up these incidents as proof of life beyond the grave. Though certainly some have experienced the feeling of well-being, will doctors verify that this is the universal report of all who have been restored to life after clinical death? The truth is that many testify they suffered unpleasantness, fear, almost panic.

Another observation is that the people reporting these stories were not dead in the full sense of the term. Clinical death involves the absence of vital life signs, but resuscitation may occur. In real death, however, there is the separation of soul from body. In the cases related, their souls had not left their bodies, or else it would have been impossible to revive them.

Mr. Bayly, who has participated with Dr. Kubler-Ross in seminars on death and dying because of his own personal loss of three children, suggests that these persons may have had an experience something like a drug high "which can produce a pseudo-dematerialization experience, a feeling of leaving the body and floating over the ocean, etc." (*Eternity* in "Out of My Mind" column, March 1976, pp. 65-66).

Mr. Bayly's reservations are well taken. Universal pleasantness at death runs counter to what Jesus taught. In the story of the rich man and the beggar Lazarus, though Lazarus at death was carried by angels into Abraham's bosom, the rich man found himself tormented in hell, certainly not a pleasant experience.

For a Christian, the compelling evidence for life after death is found in Scripture, and the most conclusive example is the bodily resurrection of Jesus Christ, the only person who ever came back to life from death, never to die again.

At the deaths of the patriarchs Abraham, Isaac, and Jacob, the Bible says that "they were gathered unto their people," which seems to indicate some type of reunion. It is also significant that in every case this phrase is distinguished from the act of burial (Gen. 25:8-9; 35:29; 49:29, 31, 33).

Later in the Old Testament, when David's baby died, the King's grief was diminished by the thought that though the infant could not return to him, "I shall go to him" (2 Sam. 12:23).

The Old Testament, though less clearly delineating the doctrine of immortality than the New Testament, nevertheless speaks several times of the resurrection of the body (Job 19:25-27; Dan. 12:2; Hosea 13:14).

When we come to the four Gospels we find Jesus' statements of a world to come, a day of judgment, everlasting life, reward in heaven, and torment in hell (Matt. 12:32, 36; 19:29; John 11:25; Matt. 10:42, 28; 13:41-42, 49-50; 25:46).

Jesus declared Abraham, Isaac, and Jacob alive by affirming that their God was not the God of the dead, but of the living (Matt. 22:31-32).

To the dying thief Jesus said, "Today shalt thou be with Me in paradise" (Luke 23:43).

The night before He died, Jesus said He would no more drink of the fruit of the vine "until that day when I drink it new with you in My Father's kingdom" (Matt. 26:29).

Following the same line of thought, the Apostle Paul, facing Nero's judgment seat, knew the alternatives before him: acquittal or death. Freedom, he said, would permit his needed ministry to the churches. But his desire was to "depart, and to be with Christ," a life beyond the grave which he called "far better" (Phil. 1:23).

In the same vein, life after death is repeatedly affirmed in the Book of Revelation (7:13-17; 14:13; 20:11-15).

An easily overlooked hint at immortality is found in the story of Job. Through disaster he lost 7,000 sheep, 3,000 camels, 500 yoke of oxen, and 500 female donkeys. More tragically he lost 10 children (7 sons and 3 daughters). But when the story ends he is blessed with double his livestock: 14,000 sheep, 6,000 camels, 1,000 yoke of oxen, and 1,000 female donkeys. But he is only blessed with the same number of children he lost: 10 in all, 7 sons and 3 daughters. Why didn't Job receive 20 children, twice the number he lost, since he ended up with double everything else? The subtle suggestion is—he didn't really lose the first 10 children for they were safe in the world to come. Thus when all his family finally reached heaven, Job had double the number of children too.

The reality of life beyond the grave should make every one of us ponder our eternal destination, because the Bible teaches only two possibilities, heaven and hell.

We take care to provide for the relatively short span of retirement after 65. How foolish not to plan for the endless ages of eternity. Confrontation with what comes after death caused one young man to prepare for the hereafter by receiving Jesus Christ as his Saviour. He was looking at a large estate one day and said to a friend, "Oh, if I were lucky enough to call this estate mine, I should be a happy fellow. It's worth a quarter million."

"And then?" said his friend.

"Why, then I'd pull down the old house and build a mansion, have lots of friends around me, get married, have several fine cars and keep the finest horses and dogs in the country."

"And then?"

"Then I would hunt, and ride, and fish, and keep open house, and enjoy life gloriously."

"And then?"

"Why, then, I suppose like other people, I should grow old and not care so much for these things."

"And then?"

"Why, in the course of nature I should die."

"And then?"

"Oh, bother your 'and then.' I have no time for you now!"

Years later the friend was surprised to hear from him, "God bless you. I owe my happiness to you."

"How?"

"By two words asked at the right time—'And then?' "

10

Will the Dead Live Again?

Within hours of his death in 1968, the body of a 24-year-old man from the New York City area was infused with an antifreeze solution, packed with dry ice, then placed in a Cryo-Capsule—a giant, heavily insulated bottle with a liquid-nitrogen-cooled interior kept at a temperature of $-200°$ F. There his corpse was to wait the day when science would discover a cure for his fatal illness. Then, according to plans, he would be thawed, cured, and restored to life. The young man was a member of the Cryonics Society, whose slogan is "Freeze, Wait, Reanimate."

The boy's mother made this tragically significant comment, "I have only a remote hope for my boy's resurrection." In contrast to this faint expectation is the absolute assurance of God's Word concerning something far better that will happen to the bodies of believers someday. Because of Christ's victory over the grave, millions affirm the words of the Apostles' Creed, "I believe in . . . the resurrection of the body."

This article of faith advances far beyond belief in the immortality of the soul. Even heathen philosophers believed in the immortality of the soul, but the resurrection of the body was another matter. The pagans on Mars Hill gave Paul respectful attention until he mentioned the raising of Jesus from the dead. But the moment "they heard of the resurrection of the dead, some mocked: and others said, 'We will hear thee again of this matter' " (Acts 17:32). They accepted the soul's immortality, a topic Plato had propounded on that very spot four centuries previously, but they would not entertain the thought of a body raised. Job asked, centuries before Christ, "If a man die, shall he live again?" (14:14)

How terminal death seems! Time and time again death comes to a loved one or friend, forcing us to make that trip to the cemetery to lay him or her away with such seeming finality. How impossible, it seems, to raise a body which surely disintegrates into dust. An archaeologist, breaking into an underground tomb saw on the ledge of a rock, for one fleeting second, the body of a beautiful girl, dressed in grave clothes. Immediately, because of the inrush of air, the body dissolved into a cloud of yellow dust. Brushing his hand along the ledge, the archaeologist scooped up all that had been the body of a human being, a handful of dust.

Skeptics ask, "How could that little pile of dust be resurrected into the girl's body?" Philosopher Pascal replies, "What right have they to say that one cannot rise from the dead? Which is more difficult, to be born or to rise again; that which has never been, be, or that which has been, be again? Is it more difficult to come into being than to return to being? Custom makes the one seem easy, the absence of custom makes the other seem impossible." If God can make a baby in the first place out of something so small as a sperm and ovum, cannot He reform our body a second time out of a teaspoon of dust?

Because amazement often greets the thought of resurrected corpses, Jesus prefaced one of His statements with, "Marvel not at this." Then He proceeded, "For the hour is coming, in the which all that are in the graves shall hear His voice, and shall come forth; they that have done good, unto the resurrection of life; and they that have done evil, unto the resurrection of damnation" (John 5:28-29).

The Intermediate State

At death, man's body remains on earth while his soul survives in a conscious state. Because man is both material body and immaterial soul functioning in this life in interacting unity, the soul after death continues in an incomplete existence until rejoined by the resurrected body. This stage between death and resurrection, known as the intermediate state, is not ideal, because man, to be complete, requires his body. Man is not a soul incidentally using a body, but he is soul and body. Paul implies that in his intermediate state man is "unclothed" (2 Cor. 5:4).

The body receives honorable emphasis in the biblical scheme. God created the body. Death is abnormal, for the soul and body were never meant to be separated. When sin and death entered the race, God set into operation His plan to rescue both soul and body. To redeem us, Christ assumed a human body, was crucified in His body (for you cannot crucify a spirit), rose bodily, makes our bodies His temple, will return bodily, at which time He will fashion our bodies like His glorious body (Phil. 3:20-21). We shall be transformed into His image, not only morally but, in some ways, physically. Though at death the soul is glorified, man remains incomplete in the intermediate state until united with his perfect body. The noted Bible teacher, Dr. Harry Ironside, used to say he didn't want an expensive tombstone, just a plain marker reading, "Saved by grace, moved out until renovated and repaired."

The soul is conscious in the intermediate state, as is shown by the requests of those who have passed on, such as the tormented rich man in the story told by Jesus (Luke 16:19-31), and by the cries of vengeance from the souls who had been slain for their testimony (Rev. 6:9-10). The consciousness of souls refutes the doctrine of soul sleep, which teaches that the soul sleeps from death to the day of resurrection. When the Bible speaks of the sleep of death, it refers, not to the soul, but to the body, since in death the body takes on the appearance of one who is asleep. Nowhere does the Bible teach that the soul ever passes into unconsciousness or sleep.

Nor does the Bible teach the existence of purgatory, a place designed to purify and fit the departed for the bliss of heaven. The Bible teaches two abodes for the dead. In the intermediate state the believer is in a condition of blessedness, with Christ, and far better off than in this life (Phil. 1:23). The wicked are in torment, as in the case of the rich man who mistreated the beggar Lazarus (Luke 16:23). These two are the only alternatives. As the Constitution of the Presbyterian Church in the United States once expressed it, "Besides these two places for souls separated from their bodies the Scripture acknowledgeth none."

Since the intermediate state continues to the resurrection day at the Second Coming, some have waited in this incomplete state for many centuries. One writer makes the interesting suggestion that the departed soul may not be "subject to time and space as we experience it in the body. There may well be another time scale to which it is subject, though we cannot say what this is. The intermediate state may seem of a very different length when measured by this other scale. In fact, it would not be surprising if, for some people at least, the Second Coming seems to follow almost directly after death, because they are now in such a different time sequence . . . and it would give point to the strong expectations of the first Christians, and even to certain words of Christ, that the Second Coming would occur almost immediately" (J. Stafford Wright, *Man in the Process of Time,* Eerdmans, p. 179).

Biblical Evidence

The Sunday after his wife was buried, a preacher began his sermon by removing his Bible from the pulpit to a chair, then asking in solemn tone, "Is there victory over death? Will I see my wife again? O science, I call you to answer." After several seconds of silence he addressed a challenge to another area, "O philosophy, I ask you to answer." After another pause he picked up his Bible, placed it on the pulpit, then firmly declared, "O Bible, you will answer." Then he read several passages which promise the resurrection.

This truth has been the constant, undying faith of saints of all times, including Abraham, Job, David, Isaiah, Daniel, and Hosea (Gen. 22; Heb. 11:19; Job 19:26; Ps. 16:9-11; Isa. 26:19;

Dan. 12:2; Hosea 13:14). Jesus claimed His voice would one day raise all dead (John 5:28-29). The bodily resurrection of Christ was the climactic point of all apostolic preaching, beginning with Peter's Pentecost sermon (Acts 2:27-32; 3:15; 4:2, 10, 33; 5:31; 10:40; 13:30-37; 17:3, 31; 26:8, 23). Paul devoted an entire chapter to the subject (1 Cor. 15).

Though Christ was the first-fruit of those who sleep, that is, the first person to return from the dead in a glorified body never to die again, both Old and New Testaments record resurrections of people, which were foreshadowings of the resurrection yet to be. Elijah and Elisha were involved in three raisings (1 Kings 17:21-22; 2 Kings 4:34-35; 13:21). Christ raised three individuals, each case older and dead longer than the previous: Jairus' 12-year-old daughter, the widow of Nain's youthful son, and Lazarus (Mark 5:42; Luke 7:14-15; John 11:44). At Jesus' resurrection many saints rose bodily from their tombs and appeared in Jerusalem (Matt. 27:52-53). Peter raised Dorcas, unselfish seamstress of Joppa (Acts 9:40-41).

What Will the Resurrection Body Be Like?

A question that crops up in every age was asked by the early Corinthian church, "What will the raised body be like?" Paul makes several statements in answer (1 Cor. 15:35-50). First, to show that the resurrected body will be similar to, yet different from, the one we had on earth, he uses the analogy of the seed and its full-grown grain. The grain that comes up is the same kind as the seed that is sown. If wheat is sown, wheat will grow, because continuity exists between that which is sown and that which comes up. Similarly, continuity will exist between the body of the believer buried in the ground and his new body that will be raised, thus making recognition and reunion possible. When a man asked if he would know his wife in heaven, the answer came, "You know her here. Do you think you shall know less in heaven than on earth?" Because of connecting similarity between present and glorified bodies, we shall know each other.

But also, just as differences exist between seed and full-grown grain, so dissimilarity will exist between our present and glorified bodies. Perhaps this is why recognition of Christ's resurrected body in his post-Easter appearances was not always immediate. Four contrasts are mentioned.

First, the body is sown in corruption but is raised in incorruption. The earthly body gets disease, dies, and decays. But the process will be reversed in the resurrection body for sickness, infirmity, and death will be eliminated (Luke 20:36).

Second, the body is sown in dishonor but is raised in glory. This body, now the vehicle through which Adamic depravity operates, will be raised a glorious body, rid forever of temptation and sin.

Third, it is sown in weakness but is raised in power. The strongest athlete must get his rest, and will ultimately lose vim, vigor, and vitality. But someday every saint will have a body of dynamic power. A lame martyr, about to be burned at the stake, threw away his crutch.

Fourth, the body is sown as a natural body but is raised a spiritual body. Our present body is controlled by our human nature, which though regenerated still retains the old Adam. The raised body will be completely dominated by our fully renewed spirit.

Incidentally, contrary to the teaching of some cults, the marriage relationship as we know it will not exist. Said Jesus of those obtaining the resurrection from the dead, they "neither marry, nor are given in marriage" (Luke 20:35).

A Body like Jesus'

Since our bodies are to be fashioned like unto Christ's glorious body, we may learn what they will be like through contemplation of His risen body. Christ was recognizable, and He could be touched, appearing to His disciples as flesh and bones, and bearing scars (John 20:27; Luke 24:39). He could be sufficiently material to eat food, though food was not necessary to His continued existence (Luke 24:41-43). He possessed wondrous agility, seen one moment, then vanishing, passing through closed doors, traveling with speed from place to place. In our glorified bodies, believers will be able to keep pace with angels, and without the burden of space suits and rocket capsules. A bulletin outside a Kentucky church read, "Traveling to outer space? Instructions inside."

Interestingly, in the 19th century, corpses were kept three days as a reminder of the three days Christ rested in the grave, then were buried with feet pointing to the east (sunrise) because of the certainty of the resurrection from the dead.

The Fountain of Youth

An advertisement aimed at women asked, "Do you look like your mother too soon?" Ponce de Leon wasn't the first or the last to search for the fountain of youth. Man doesn't wish to grow old, but despite vitamins, Geritol, and cold cream, wrinkles come, hair turns gray or disappears, teeth decay, limbs tremble, and memories shorten. The five Bs of ongoing age make their appearance: bifocals, bridges, bunions, baldness, and bulges.

However, the quest for perpetual youth finds its answer in the resurrected body. At the tomb of Jesus, on that resurrection morning, sat a young man (Mark 16:5). Though really an angel, he took the form of a man whose youthfulness impressed the disciples. May not the youth of the visitor from the eternal realm suggest that creatures in the world to come will appear as in the prime of life? Because Christ was 33 years of age at the time of His resurrection, some surmise that our glorified bodies will give the appearance of thirtyish.

Not only will our glorified bodies be young in appearance, but in strength as well. Most athletes are young. As age creeps up, muscles and reflexes refuse to respond as quickly, and energy declines. As one person wrote:

> How do I know my youth is all spent?
> Well, my get-up-and-go has got up and went.
> But in spite of it all, I am able to grin,
> When I think of the places my get-up has been.
> Old age is golden, so I've heard it said,
> But sometimes I wonder as I get into bed.
> With my ears in a drawer, my teeth in a cup,
> My eyes on the table, until I wake up.

Ere sleep dims my eyes, I say to myself,
Is there anything else I should put on the shelf?
When I was young my slippers were red,
I could kick up my heels right over my head.
When I grew older, my slippers were blue,
But still I could dance the whole night through.
Now that I'm old, my slippers are black,
I walk to the store and I puff my way back.
The reason I know my youth is all spent,
My get-up-and-go has got up and went.
But I really don't mind, and I think with a grin
Of all the places my get-up has been.
Since I have retired from life's competition,
I busy myself with complete repetition,
I get up each morning, dust off my wits,
Pick up my paper and read the obits.
If my name is still missing, I know I'm not dead.
So I eat a good breakfast and go back to bed.

Author unknown

The young man by the tomb had just exercised superhuman strength in rolling back the heavy stone (Matt. 28:2). Someday we shall surpass angels in strength. All deformities and deficiencies of the present body will be erased. Gone will be aches of the aged, pains of the paralyzed, panting of cardiacs, puffing of emphysema victims, hospitals, medicines, ambulances, crutches, and glasses. Everyone will be rejuvenated with permanent health and boundless vitality.

As theologian William Newton Clarke neared the sunset of life, a friend suggested the sadness of one so vigorous coming to the feebleness of age. But Clarke would have none of it, but rather full of faith wrote:

Gone, they tell me is youth,
Gone the strength of my life.
Nothing remains but decline,
Nothing but age and decay.
Not so! I am God's little child,
Only beginning to live.

Coming the days of my prime,
Coming the strength of my life,
Coming the vision of God,
Coming my bloom and my power.

A little caterpillar groveling along the ground bemoaned, "How close to the earth I keep and creep. Would I could rise with outspread wings, like a butterfly, and float over field and meadow to behold beauties I cannot imagine." One day the caterpillar found itself in a hard shell provided by nature. Sometime later it awoke to a new existence, threw off its chrysalis, then borne aloft by brilliantly hued wings, skimmed over field and meadow, moving among fragrant flowers, no longer confined to the dust of earth. The transformation of our body of humiliation into our promised glorious body will be unimaginably far more momentous.

When Is the Body Raised?

At the second coming of Christ, at the last trump, in a moment, in the twinkling of an eye, the dead shall be raised incorruptible, and living saints shall be changed, without dying, to receive an incorruptible body (1 Cor. 15:51-53). Paul wrote, "The Lord Himself shall descend from heaven with a shout, with the voice of the archangel, and with the trump of God: and the dead in Christ shall rise first. Then we which are alive and remain shall be caught up together with them in the clouds, to meet the Lord in the air: and so shall we ever be with the Lord" (1 Thes. 4:16-17).

A visitor to a Japanese island discovered a grave where several Christians had been buried. However, before burial they had been beheaded, their heads buried on another island. An early missionary had taught that Christians would rise from the dead at the coming of Christ, so to keep this from happening, persecuting officials separated heads from bodies. But they erred, not knowing the power of God which will be demonstrated on the resurrection day.

When C. H. Spurgeon read a gift copy of Andrew Bonar's commentary on Leviticus, he was so blessed that he returned the book with the request that Dr. Bonar place therein both his autograph and photograph. Bonar returned the book with this note, "Dear Spurgeon: Here is the book with my autograph and my photograph. Had you been willing to wait a short season, you could have had a better likeness, for I shall be like Him when I shall see Him as He is." This likeness will be stamped on all believers when Christ appears at His second coming (1 John 3:3).

Though some believe in one general resurrection of both saved and unsaved at the same time, others teach that the non-Christian dead will not be raised till a thousand years after the resurrection of the saved, citing, "But the rest of the dead lived not again until the thousand years were finished. This is the first resurrection. Blessed and holy is he that hath part in the first resurrection" (Rev. 20:5-6). Whether the unsaved are raised at the same time or a thousand years later, theirs is a resurrection to face judgment and damnation. To have a glorious resurrection with a body like Christ, we must receive Him as our Saviour in this life.

One day a workman accidentally dropped a beautiful silver cup into an acid bath. Confused and afraid, because both the cup and its beauty were destroyed by the acid, he ran, shamefacedly to his foreman. How could they replace it? The foreman was equal to the occasion. Going to the vat containing the acid that had disintegrated the silver cup, he put in a reagent. Soon the silver of the cup was recaptured from the acid—in a shapeless lump, to be sure. Then the foreman employed a silversmith to remold the mass into a cup far more beautiful than the original. So shall it be with our bodies at the resurrection.

We don't need deep-freeze capsules to house our frozen corpses for later reanimation when a cure has been discovered for whatever disease ends our physical life. Rather, when we belong to the One who said, "I am He that liveth, and was dead; and, behold, I am alive for evermore, Amen; and have the keys of hell and of death" (Rev. 1:18), we can triumphantly shout:

> O death, where is thy sting?
> O grave, where is thy victory?

11

Should We Believe in Heaven and Hell?

On display in Abercrombie and Fitch's New York City department store is a barometer which had been delivered to a Long Island home on the morning of September 21, 1938. The owner was quite disappointed to find the needle stuck at hurricane. No matter how forcibly he shook the barometer, the needle returned to the storm position. So, writing a stuffy letter to Abercrombie and Fitch, he went outside and mailed it. Later that day a severe hurricane struck Long Island, doing considerable damage to his home. The barometer had been right.

People ask, "Does hell really exist, or is all the heaven and hell we get down here in this life?" The barometer of God's Word says judgment is coming.

Judgment
Man seems to possess an innate idea of a day of reckoning. This inborn conviction is mentioned in the final verse of Ecclesiastes, a book which reflects the best reasoning of natural man, "For God shall bring every work into judgment, with every secret thing, whether it be good, or whether it be evil" (12:14).

The injustice of this present order demands a day of judgment. How often the righteous suffer while the wicked prosper. Tyrants sit on thrones while heroes die in dungeons. At the Dachau concentration camp today a guide may point out the location where Pastor Niemoeller was imprisoned, while Hitler's forces ran rampant over much of Europe. But one day the tables reversed. Niemoeller was freed but Hitler committed suicide. Sometimes the wicked flourish to their dying day and the godly barely eke out an existence. How, then, a thinking person may ask, can justice be administered and rewards doled out unless a day of judgment lies ahead?

Jesus spoke of a coming reversal of conditions when the poor would be rich, and the rich poor; when the hungry would be filled, and the full hungry; when the weeping would laugh, and the laughing would weep (Luke 6:20-26). Jesus' many warnings of coming judgment were solemn and searching. "In twelve out of thirty-six of His parables He depicts men as judged, condemned, and punished for their sins" (Fred Carl Kuehner, "Heaven or Hell?" *Christianity Today,* July 5, 1968). Repeatedly He spoke of a day of judgment (Matt. 11:22, 24; 12:36, 42).

The day has already been fixed. According to Paul, God "hath appointed a day, in the which He will judge the world" (Acts 17:31). The date has already been scheduled on the divine calendar. The idea of a final tribunal did not originate in the gross descriptions of medieval writers and artists who depicted writhing souls in torturous flame, but stems from the joint testimony of both Old and New Testaments. The writer of Hebrews lists "eternal judgment" among the elementary doctrines of Christ (Heb. 6:1-2).

People may evade God in this life, but after death all roads lead by His throne. "It is appointed unto men once to die, but after this the judgment" (Heb. 9:27).

The judge will be none other than the Lord Jesus Christ Himself (John 5:22-23, 27; 2 Tim. 4:1; Acts 10:42). The Man on the cross becomes the Man on the throne. "The texts which speak of God as judging the world are to be understood as referring to God the Son. No appeal can be made from the Son to the Father" (William Evans, *The Great Doctrines of the Bible,* Moody Press, 1939, p. 253). He will be involved in at least two major categories of judgment: the judgment of believers, and the judgment of unbelievers.

The Judgment of Believers. Believers will never face judgment for their sins. Christ bore the penalty of our iniquities on the cross. Believers will be judged not for their sins, but for their works. Paul declared, "For we must all appear before the judgment seat of Christ; that every one may receive the things done in his body, according to that he hath done, whether it be good or bad" (2 Cor. 5:10). Paul also warned that our works will be tested by fire to see if they are gold, silver, precious stones, or wood, hay, or stubble. The believer whose work remains will be rewarded. The one whose work is burned will suffer loss, though he personally will be saved, "yet so as by fire" (1 Cor. 3:11-15).

More than one sermon has been titled, "Tears in Heaven," based on the premise that when the judgment seat of Christ reveals wasted time, treasure, talent, and talk, deep remorse will be experienced for what should have been and was not. John warned against losing a full reward (2 John 8). But faithfulness in our Christian life will bring the Master's commendation, "Well done, thou good and faithful servant" (Matt. 25:21).

The Judgment of Unbelievers. Toward the close of the Bible we have the graphic description of the Great White Throne judgment. Judged for their sinful deeds, the subjects are cast into the lake of fire (Rev. 20:11-15).

The One who is willing to be the Saviour now will become the Judge of those who reject Him. The same sun that helps the grass to grow also withers the grass. The same ocean, the buoyancy of which keeps ships afloat, will dash other ships to pieces.

A promising young man became an alcoholic. His father's friend, a lawyer, gave the lad some kindly advice, which the boy laughed off. Weeks later, the lawyer spotted the boy staggering across a busy street with a car fast bearing down on him. The lawyer pushed him to safety in the nick of time, again warned him, and again received a laugh in return. Years passed, and a middle-aged man on trial for murder was found guilty. Asked by the judge if he had anything to say, a ray of recognition dawned on him. He jumped to his feet and said, "Yes, I do have something to say. Your honor, I recognize you as an old friend of my father. Once you saved my life, and I believe you are going to do it again." The judge replied, "True, my boy, I'm a friend of your father. I did save your life, but I'm your judge now. And I must find you guilty and pass sentence on you."

In the day of judgment, unbelievers who rejected the Gospel may hear the Judge say, "I was willing to be your Saviour then. But I'm your Judge now, and I must pass sentence. Depart from me into everlasting punishment."

Hell

A lady said to a minister, "I didn't like listening to your sermon on hell tonight." Whereupon he replied, "And I didn't like preaching it."

Many do not believe in the existence of hell. Others, who do, rarely preach on it, or do so reluctantly. Some have resorted to espousing the annihilation of the wicked, or the ultimate salvation of all. Unbelievers use the word *hell* glibly in conversation on the street, in the news media, and in literature. Though perverted through popular profanity, *hell* is a scriptural term found as much in the teachings of Christ as elsewhere in the Bible.

"The strongest support of the doctrine of Endless Punishment is the teaching of Christ, the Redeemer of man. . . . The mere perusal of Christ's words when He was upon earth, without note or comment upon them, will convince the unprejudiced that the Redeemer of sinners knew and believed that for impenitent men and devils there is an endless punishment" (William Shedd, *The Doctrine of Endless Punishment,* Scribners, 1887, p. 12). To reinforce his statement, Shedd took three pages to quote the words of Christ, citing such passages as Matthew 7:22-23; 10:28; 11:23; Mark 9:43-48; Luke 9:25; 12:9-10, 46; 16:22-23; John 5:28-29; 8:21.

Jesus didn't coddle His generation by a soft teaching on hell. If He believed in its existence, that should be enough for us to accept its reality. Hell's awfulness is demonstrated by the fact that Jesus left heaven to suffer on the cross and provide us a way of escape.

Owners of a Las Vegas night club named "Hell Incorporated" erected signs along the highway from Los Angeles, reading, "This is the road to Hell," and "Hell is fun." New Testament signposts say the following about hell: It is a place of weeping and gnashing of teeth (Matt. 8:12); a place of crying for mercy (Luke 16:24); a place of torment (Luke 16:23); a place of unquenchable fire (Mark 9:48); a place of darkness (Rev. 9:2); a place of imprisonment (2 Peter 2:4); a place without rest (Rev. 14:11); a place for the wicked (Rev. 22:15); a place of pain (Rev. 16:10); a place of eternal damnation (Mark 3:29); a place where God's wrath is poured out (Rev. 14:10); a place of everlasting destruction (2 Thes. 1:9); a place of finality (Luke 16:26).

The pictures conjured by these passages raise profound questions, which should not be aggravated by insisting that these terms be pressed to their full literal significance. Christian doctrine has never required that "unquenchable fire" be interpreted as a fiery oven with raging flame, as some older divines have done. Charles Hodge, respected Princeton theologian, wrote, "There seems no more reason for supposing that the fire spoken of in Scripture is to be a literal fire, than that the worm that never dies is literally a worm. The devil and his angels who are to suffer the vengeance of eternal fire, and whose doom the finally impenitent are to share, have no material bodies to be acted upon by elemental fire" (*Systematic Theology,* III, Scribners, 1876, p. 868).

Though opposed to a literal interpretation of the terms used to describe hell, Hodge is not denying one iota of the reality of hell as a place of eternal punishment, nor is he minimizing the misery and suffering of those forever cut off from Christ.

Some hold that the undying worm and the unquenchable fire suggest, as a minimum, the relentless gnawings of conscience and the perpetual insatiability of desire. Jude speaks of punishment in terms of "wandering stars, to whom is reserved the blackness of darkness forever" (v. 13). One explanation, trying to combine the seemingly mutually exclusive figures of fire and darkness, places the lake of fire on some star whirling in the endless blackness of outer space. What can be agreed is that all the terms point to something which C. S. Lewis calls "unspeakably horrible."

Spandau Prison, a grim brick fortress on the western outskirts of Berlin, confines the seven major Nazi war criminals sentenced at the Nuremberg Trials to terms ranging from 10 years to life. One of them, Albert Speer, Hitler's master technocrat of the Nazi war effort and overseer of 2 million slave laborers, wrote a book describing life there (*Spandau,* Macmillan & Co., 1976). The seven prisoners, the only inmates since World War II, were forbidden to speak to one another, were addressed by number only, never by name, could not touch anyone, not even their wives during brief and heavily supervised visits. Presents judged too luxurious were rejected.

The demented and emaciated Rudolph Hess often moaned all night that guards had poisoned his milk. Another prisoner, Grand Admiral Raeder, imitated Hess' moans just to annoy him. All had to mop floors.

Haunted by the waste of his life, Speer survived partly by persisting in a series of elaborate games, creations he called "the organization of emptiness." He conducted experiments to see if peas could be made to grow sideways. Brooding over buildings he would never construct, he made an exhaustive study of windows, figuring out the price of light per square yard in terms of labor per hour.

Could this frustrating, meaningless, lonely, conscience-tormenting existence be a little foretaste of hell? Speer wrote that boredom was one torment that Dante forgot.

Hell is logical. Punishment is basically retributive. No person should be punished unless he deserves to be, certainly never merely to reform him or deter others. If asked how a saint could possibly enjoy heaven knowing people were in hell, it could be pointed out that God has this knowledge, yet maintains His joy in heaven. Certainly He is not less merciful than man.

Hell's duration is forever. Christ concludes the parable of the sheep and the goats, "And these [the cursed] shall go away into everlasting punishment: but the righteous into life eternal" (Matt. 25:46). *Everlasting* and *eternal* are the same word in the original.

As long as heaven is, so is hell. To deny the permanence of hell is impossible without also removing the permanence of heaven. The balanced phrases require the same length of time for both.

This doctrine ought to mellow our hearts for those headed for a lost eternity. Two preachers candidated on successive Sundays for a vacant pulpit. Both spoke on hell, but one was chosen by unanimous vote. The reason: the other preacher seemed not to care if people were going there; the successful candidate spoke as if he hoped no one would end up there.

Many views try to explain away or bypass hell. One attempt is annihilation, which says that the righteous will live eternally, but the wicked will be judged and destroyed. Also known as conditional immortality, this viewpoint explains "punished with everlasting destruction" (2 Thes. 1:9) as referring to the result of punishment (annihilation) and not to the punishment itself. This interpretation cannot be maintained by sound exegesis.

What purpose is the resurrection if the lost are to be extinguished forever? How can it be punishment if the object is unconscious, for no such thing exists as unconscious punishment? The references to the retribution of the wicked, fire, worm, and eternal darkness, cannot be applied to a condition of annihilation. The parallel between eternal life and eternal punishment fails if the fate of the impenitent is extinction.

Another attempted route to bypass hell is universalism, which teaches that all humanity will ultimately be saved. The 19th century saw strong impetus for the universalist position, including an American denomination whose very name showed its espousal of this doctrine, the Universalist Church. Poets of that era expressed what Tennyson called "the larger hope," a belief in a redemptive mercy that would eventually include all mankind.

In our day universalism has found a welcome in most major denominations. The real missionary message, which tells men they need to be saved, is changed in universalistic theology, to inform people they are already saved. Men need not repent, for the universal Saviour is already there. It's not, "Be ye reconciled," but "Ye are already reconciled."

Universalism forgets that the most famous verse in the Bible implies the possibility of being lost. "Should not perish" has been called "the dark line" of John 3:16. Universalism emphasizes the love of God while forgetting the justice of God. A loving God saved Noah and his family, but a holy God rained down a destroying flood on the rest of humanity. A loving God has provided a way of escape through the cross for all who exercise faith in Christ, but a holy God will someday say to the unrepentant, "Depart from me into everlasting fire."

Universalism quotes verses to support its position, but forgets other verses, often in the same context, which contradict its viewpoint. For example, universalists quote Paul's statement that "every tongue [shall] confess that Jesus Christ is Lord" (Phil. 2:11), but then neglect a later passage that asserts that the destination of enemies of the cross will be "destruction" (3:19).

If hell does not exist, or if no one is going there, what need is there for evangelism? On an American troop ship the soldiers crowded around their chaplain, asking, "Do you believe in hell?" When he answered no, they replied, "Well, will you please resign? For if there is no hell, we do not need you, and if there is a hell, we do not wish to be led astray!"

Heaven

What is heaven like? Is it lounging around on Cloud Nine, strumming away on our harps? The problem that confronts us, as with the topic of hell, is the literalness of New Jerusalem's jasper wall, foundations of precious stones, pearly gates, and golden streets like transparent glass. Behind the dimensions of the city, the value of the gems, and all the picturesque language, what can we say about heaven?

Heaven is a place. Heaven is not a figment of our imagination, not the projection of our wishes, not absorption into nothingness, but a blessed reality. Jesus said, "I go to prepare a place for you" (John 14:2). Distinct from the first heaven or atmospheric blanket of air which extends a few miles from the earth, and distinct from the second heaven or celestial sky in which sun, moon, and stars appear, heaven was called by Paul "the third heaven" (2 Cor. 12:2). In heaven the nature of space, time, and matter will likely be different. Heaven may be closer to us than we realize.

A delightful place. Running through literature is a conviction that man is a homeless wanderer on a pilgrimage through unfriendly territory, haunted by memories of a former Edenic glory, with also a deep longing to return. Heaven will answer this deep-seated desire for a utopian existence.

The lovely sights, smells, sounds, and other sensations of earth may be a little foretaste of heaven. Unimaginable color, beauty, and symphony await us. Scott Carpenter, the second American to circle the earth in space, reported that the "colors glowed vigorously alive with light." Then he told how he watched the band of sunset narrow "until nothing was left but a rim of blue." He called the experience all but supernatural.

Joy will abound. Thrilling tasks and fantastic folks will eliminate all depression and boredom. The freedom of the abundant life, fully possible only in the glorified state, will be ours. The Psalmist's statement will be fulfilled, "In thy presence is fulness of joy; at thy right hand there are pleasures forevermore" (16:11).

A little girl, gazing up at the lovely, star-studded sky, exclaimed, "If the wrong side of heaven is so beautiful, what must the right side be like!"

A busy place. Though our knowledge may be advanced in this life, in heaven we shall probably still be learning. Heaven will not be a colony for the lazy. God's "servants shall serve Him" (Rev. 22:3). May not part of our duty be to have dominion over some area of God's kingdoms? Jesus spoke of a faithful servant hearing, "Well done, thou good and faithful servant; thou hast been faithful over a few things, I will make thee ruler over many things; enter thou into the joy of thy Lord" (Matt. 25:21).

But isn't heaven supposed to be a place of rest, a never ending vacation where we recline in pleasant groves by flowery banks to while away eternity? Combining the concepts of labor and rest, may heaven not be a place of constructive activity in serving Christ without frustration and wearisome toil, thus resulting in pleasurable, restful labor? "No longer tedium, but Te Deum."

A place filled with musical worship. The Old Testament puts much emphasis on music, beginning with the song of Moses after the triumphant crossing of the Red Sea right through to the choirs and instruments of Solomon's temple. So does the New Testament, from the angelic chorus at Jesus' birth to the choirs of heaven singing praises to the Lamb (Rev. 19:1). The opening program at a recent National Religious Broadcasters' convention in Washington, D.C., featured an array of America's finest gospel artists in a musical program, which lasted from 7 P.M. till after 11 P.M., leading one attendee to remark, "I wonder if this is what heaven will be like." Neither traditional choir nor folk group with electronic accompaniment, heaven's music will far surpass anything we can dream of hearing. This music will focus adoration on the Son of God whose glory illumines the holy city.

An exclusive place. The irritations of life will be absent in heaven: dentures, poor eyesight, financial pressures, for the former things are passed away (Rev. 21:4).

With tongue in cheek; comedian H. Allen Smith in an article, "My Requirements of Heaven," listed items he wanted in the world to come, including an uncensored copy of every book ever written, a reel of every motion picture ever produced, a tape of every TV program, a rerun of every stage play from the ancient Greeks down to modern Broadway, plus a battalion of beautiful girls at his beck and call. (*New York Times Magazine,* March 14, 1976, p. 111) The comedian should have read the list of persons and things excluded from heaven. "And there shall in no wise enter into it anything that defileth, neither whatsoever worketh abomination, or maketh a lie" (Rev. 21:27). The Bible's final chapter says, "Without are dogs, and sorcerers, and whoremongers and murderers, and idolaters, and whosoever loveth and maketh a lie" (Rev. 22:15). Under these exclusions much on the comedian's list would never be admitted. Heaven is a place of holiness as suggested by the expression "holy city" (Rev. 21:2). Banned will be unrepentant unbelievers, infidels, skeptics, agnostics, atheists, and blasphemers. No sermons will be preached to sinners.

A sociable place. The redeemed of all ages will be there:

Enoch, Noah, Abraham, Isaac, Jacob, Joseph, Job, David, Isaiah, Jeremiah, Daniel, to name a few from Old Testament pages. From the New Testament we'll converse with Peter, Andrew, James, John, Matthew, Thomas and all the disciples, and a host of others including Paul, Barnabas, Timothy, Silas, Apollos, Aquila, and Priscilla. We'll be on friendly terms with great characters from church history like Augustine, Luther, Livingstone, Hudson Taylor, Spurgeon, and Moody. We'll meet the unsung martyrs of every century, including those who recently died under Communist tyranny. Our loved ones who died in Christ, whom we have long missed, will be there.

Just as Moses and Elijah, separated in history by 500 years, knew each other on the Mount of Transfiguration (Matt. 17:3), so we will not only recognize our relatives, but we will also be able to identify saints of all ages. We will be surrounded by people from all walks of life and from all denominations who have devotion to the Lord Jesus Christ in common. If fellowship on earth is significant, how much more meaningful it will be in heaven. Above all, at the center will be the Lord Jesus Christ. Without Him heaven would not be heaven.

A place for prepared people. Someone said there would be three surprises in heaven: to see some people there we didn't expect, to find some missing we expected, and to find ourselves there. But the Bible teaches that we can know in advance that we will be there. Heaven's residents will be those whose names are written in the Lamb's Book of Life (Rev. 20:15; 21:27). To have our names recorded, we must recognize that we are unfit in our natural state for a holy heaven, that we cannot earn heaven by our good works, that the Lamb of God came down to earth to pay the penalty of our sins on the cross. Then we must receive the Lamb of God as the One who died to save us from our sins and to give us eternal life. Those who so trust Christ have their names inscribed in His volume, the Lamb's Book of Life.

A man walked up to the desk of a busy Washington, D.C., hotel and received a room immediately. Standing near the desk was a traveler who had just been turned away because no room was available. The disappointed traveler asked the newcomer, "How is it that you are able to get a room, while I, here before you, could not?" The registered guest replied, "Because I sent my reservation on in advance."

By having our names entered in the Lamb's Book of Life while we are still down here, we can be like those to whom Jesus said, "Rejoice, because your names are written in heaven" (Luke 10:20).

12

Divine Masterpiece

One recent winter a professional sculptor, living in Canada, created a giant snow statue of a reclining man, leaning on his elbow, in the front yard of his home. A reporter remarked, "Unfortunately the work—16 feet long and 7 feet high—will only grace the countryside as long as the weather stays cold."

How unlike the work of the Divine Sculptor, who made real man in His own likeness. Despite the marring of God's likeness in man, the image can be restored. One day man, in Christ, will be glorified, to remain forever God's most beautiful work of art.

The Work of Art

God is the Master Artist. Nature abounds with His handiwork: azure sky with sun by day and stars by night, fleecy clouds, majestic mountains, symmetric snowflakes, vast oceans, luxuriant grass, colorful flowers, tree-dotted landscapes, and awesome deserts.

Divine artistry shows itself in the animal kingdom: graceful birds, sleek fish, and land creatures like the leopard, giraffe, and deer. Animal lore abounds with amazing feats involving the radar of bats and the return of salmon to spawn in the same fresh waters where they were hatched.

Though the plant and animal worlds reveal the creativity of our Maker, the study of man most fully displays His artistic genius. After each creative act, God said, "It is good." After creating man and woman, He could have exclaimed, "My best— my masterpiece!"

Rabbinic teaching claimed that Adam was created with a ray of divine glory on his face, later lost in the Fall. Paul may have alluded to this idea on two occasions. To the Roman Christians he wrote, "All have sinned, and come short of the glory of God" (Rom. 3:23). Contrary to most commentators who take the glory of God to mean either God's perfection or approval, the passage may well refer to the original status of man, a created glory lost through sin. In another passage, mentioning that woman was created after man, Paul stated that man "is the image and glory of God: but the woman is the glory of man" (1 Cor. 11:7). This may mean that just as man reflects the glorious perfection of God's work, so woman reflects the same glorious perfection of God's work as created from man.

Shakespeare (in *Hamlet*) exclaimed, "What a piece of work is man! how noble in reason! how infinite in faculty! in form and moving how express and admirable! in action how like an angel! in apprehension how like a god! the beauty of the world! the paragon of animals!"

But the noble work of art was marred.

The Marring of God's Masterpiece

Man did not keep his high and holy estate, but fell. Through disobedience, man became alienated from God, at odds with his fellow creatures, and disoriented within himself.

Guilt, depravity, and death became the lot of every human. Though still able to reason and invent, man lost moral mastery over himself and his environment. He has the brains to make weapons of war, but not the ethical power to control them. Consequently, the world finds itself in constant international upheaval, as well as civil strife and local crime. The trouble with our world is the sum total of all that is wrong with us as individuals.

Multitudes find no meaning in existence. Ours is a day of great restlessness, nervous tension, and rising confusion. Counselors report countless people suffering not from any psychosis, but tortured with a lack of meaning in life. Errol Flynn, legendary, swashbuckling movie star, whose movies often appear on the late show, plunged into brooding in mid-life over the purpose of existence. Finding no answers, he designed a squarish question mark which he wore sewed on his clothing like a brand. In his autobiography, *Wicked, Wicked Ways,* he wrote, "You can love every instant of living and still want to be dead." He died still seemingly branded with the mark of the unanswerable question (Review in *Time,* January 1941).

A bystander watched some young people sprawled around a cocktail lounge, chatting, laughing, and sharing pieces of information on the world situation, existential philosophy, modern literature, and best sellers. He observed that they seemed to know a lot about most every subject, except their reason for being in the barroom idling their time away. For many, life is an empty dream or nightmare.

A cartoon showed a lifeguard sitting on top of his stand marked "Lifeguard," muttering to another guard, "What is life that I should guard it?" Augustine's prayer had the answer for restive mankind, "Thou hast made us after Thine image, and our hearts can find no rest until they rest in Thee."

Other church leaders of Augustine's period, such as Cyril of Alexandria, Methodius, and Gregory of Nyssa, depict man's resemblance to God by a series of analogies drawn from sculpture and painting. They often portray the divine image in man as obscured by mud, grime, and smoke, or again, as a painting ruined by the application of wrong colors.

But despite original sin and all its consequent evils, despite greed which leads to inflation, the spread of pornography, and the declaration of war, the Christian has a fundamentally optimistic view of humanity's possibilities. Man made in God's image somehow resembles God more than does anything else in the universe. Murder is a serious offense because fallen man is still to some degree in the image of God (Gen. 9:6). How incongruous that man, made with such excellent dignity, should dissipate his high potential on smut, nastiness, or rapacity.

Over 400 years ago Michaelangelo, commissioned by the fathers of Florence to sculpt a figure of David, chose a gigantic block of marble so misshapen no other sculptor had been able to do anything with it. From that slab of marble he carved his now famous *David*. How like God Himself, who can take a disfigured block of humanity and refashion it in His own divine likeness.

The Re-creation of God's Masterpiece

The Bible can be outlined this way: *generation* in the divine likeness, *degeneration* through sin, *regeneration* through the Gospel. Or to put it another way, *creation, desecration, re-creation*.

God set out to restore the divine image. The Father had a design, the Son executed the plan, and the Spirit brings it to perfection. God sent His Son to die for man's imperfections, so that the blots and the defects on His masterpiece could be wiped away or corrected by Calvary. Forgiveness, reconciliation, justification, and cleansing, provided by God at great cost, made possible the remaking of men. Conversion, regeneration, death to the old way, and rising to a new path, point to the glorious possibility of restoration of the divine image.

The Bible calls the re-created man God's *workmanship*. The Greek word for *workmanship* gives us the word *poem* (Eph. 2:10), but can be used for any work of art. Through regeneration we are God's work of art, His poem. He can take that which is despised by others and create from it something of moral beauty.

Regeneration is followed by sanctification. Regeneration is the beginning act of the Holy Spirit in salvation by which the principle of the new life is implanted in man, and the governing disposition of the soul is made holy. Sanctification is the continuous operation of the Holy Spirit whereby the regenerate sinner is delivered from the pollution of sin, enabled to perform good works, and renewed in the image of God.

Growth is not automatic. In the battle within every Christian, the believer is to slough off the old and put on the new. His objective should coincide with the Lord's objective, which is holiness of life. Paul alluded to this struggle in his letter to the Roman Christians (Rom. 7). With his mind he wanted to serve Christ, but with his flesh he wanted to serve the old nature. Though he knew what he ought to do, he didn't do it. All believers face the same problem. Sainthood is something toward which we must strive, and which we can attain to a degree which will differentiate us from those who follow the flesh.

Sometimes the process may be painful, especially if the Master Sculptor must strike blow after blow with His mallet, or stroke after stroke with His chisel. Saintly Horatius Bonar wrote,

Great Sculptor, hew and polish us, nor let,
Hidden and lost, Thy form within us lie.
Spare not the stroke, do with us as Thou wilt;
Let there be nought unfinished, broken, marred:
Complete Thy purpose, that we may become
Thy perfect image, O our God and Lord.

Though the image will never be perfected in this life, we should progressively become more like the Master. The measure of godliness attained will come from the fulness of the Spirit who will produce His fruit in us: love, joy, peace, patience, kindness, goodness, faithfulness, meekness, self-control. These qualities are the essence of likeness to Christ, who Himself is the express image of God's person (Heb. 1:3).

As Peter became more Christlike, his vacillation gave way to stability. As John grew in grace, his thunder mellowed into gentleness. If an alcoholic, dope addict, homosexual, or prostitute becomes a Christian, we expect them to attain a high degree of mastery over their vices. Similarly a gossip, hater, or envier should gain victory over their besetting perversity. Revenge, bitterness, malice, blasphemy, backbiting, immorality, covetousness, and dishonesty should all be replaced by love, thus reflecting Christ's likeness.

Will genetic engineering play any part in the transformation of man's character into the divine image? Today scientists are pursuing startling, almost frightening experiments to discover the role of genes in human reproduction. They hope that through careful manipulation of the genes, man may radically alter future generations.

A conference of evangelical leaders was held in the summer of 1976 at Wheaton College to evaluate the moral aspects of possible genetic engineering. According to Dr. Donald MacKay of England's University of Keele, the participants agreed that though we have an obligation to do good, it should be remembered that (1) our wisdom is limited, (2) that our motives are easily warped by our sinful natures, (3) that even good aims can conflict, (4) that the achievement of material goals and improvements can all too readily crowd out the spiritual purposes of our human existence, (5) that even a well-intentioned manipulative approach may degrade human subjects, and (6) "that there are no human engineering substitutes for personal salvation, even if some [feel] that certain virtues listed as 'fruits of the Spirit' can be assisted by the kind of reinforcement [perhaps encouragement is the ordinary word for it] that behavioral psychology is beginning to understand" ("Human Engineering and the Future of Man" in *Christian Heritage,* November 1976, p. 23). Salvatory transformation will not come through genetic manipulation but through the sanctifying work of the Holy Spirit.

The growing life of liberty through the Spirit is a foretaste of greater glory yet to be. Though we have no abiding city here, God grants us a divine pledge of our future inheritance, called the "Holy Spirit of promise . . . the earnest of our inheritance" (Eph. 1:13-14). *Earnest* was a deposit paid down by a purchaser when a bargain was struck, as a kind of first installment to guarantee the rest would follow. The gift of God's Spirit is an advance foretaste and guarantee of future blessings for God's people.

Bishop Taylor Smith, once chaplain-in-chief of British armed forces, was asked by a young stranger, "Are you saved?" The bishop replied, "I am in the process of being saved." The youth, thinking the bishop's view of salvation deficient, showed surprise. Whereupon the bishop proceeded to instruct him in the grammar of salvation, explaining that in the past a transaction had been completed, in the present there is to be growing in grace, and in the future we shall be made completely in the divine image. The bishop, in essence, outlined the three tenses of salvation: believers have been saved from the penalty of sin, are being saved from its power, and will one day be saved from its very presence.

The Glorification of Man

Our salvation, begun at the new birth (regeneration) is a process (sanctification), which shall terminate in endtime perfection (glorification). As Bernard Ramm put it, "The newborn Christian in this life is to press on to maturity. But the maturity of this life will always be partial. In the end-time glorification the imperfect maturity of this life will give way to the fullness of perfection" (*Them He Glorified,* Eerdmans, 1963, p. 67).

Man's glorification, an oft-neglected topic, is repeatedly mentioned in the New Testament. The justified are to be glorified (Rom. 8:30). Believers are to "rejoice in hope of the glory of God" (Rom. 5:2), share Christ's glory (John 17:22), are called to God's kingdom and glory (1 Thes. 2:12), obtain salvation with eternal glory (2 Thes. 2:14; 2 Tim. 2:10), will be brought as sons to glory (Heb. 2:10), are called to eternal glory (1 Peter 5:10; 2 Peter 1:3). God, who is a God of glory, intends to share His glory with the crown of His creation, redeemed and restored man.

In the day of our glorification we shall be without moral blemish (Eph. 5:27), faultless (Jude 24), holy (Col. 1:22), immaculately pure and without offence (Phil. 1:10), blameless (1 Thes. 5:23), free to be true to our nature as God's children (Rom. 8:21), and conformed to the image of Jesus Christ (Rom. 8:29). Though we are now being changed into the same image from degree of glory to degree of glory by the Spirit, the final transformation will occur at the second coming of Christ. The Apostle John wrote, "When He shall appear, we shall be like Him; for we shall see Him as He is" (1 John 3:2).

A glorified man needs a glorified environment. The recording of man's creation in the first chapters in the Bible, along with the creation of the universe, shows that man is part of the physical world. Man's inner being affects the outer man (body), and beyond that, his cosmos. But the entrance of sin altered these basic harmonies. Because of the inner man's disobedience, judgment was pronounced on the outer man (body) which causes it to return to dust. Also, the physical creation was cursed ("cursed is the ground for thy sake"), so that man provides his bread by the sweat of his brow (Gen. 3:17-19).

Redemption, however, provides for the restoration of these harmonies. The inner man is regenerated and begins the process of sanctification. At the second coming of Christ the outer man will receive a glorified body. But in addition, the healing of the cosmos has been promised. Jesus spoke of a new world when He "shall sit in the throne of His glory" (Matt. 19:28).

Paul spoke of creation, subjected to futility through man's fall, groaning in travail and unable to provide man with a perfect environment. He also stated that man's body was in bondage to decay. But Paul also declared that at the glorification of the believer the corruption of bondage would be lifted, both for the human body and for creation (Rom. 8:19-23).

The renewal of the cosmos is referred to as a new heaven and a new earth (2 Peter 3:10-13; Rev. 21:1, 5). Man's redeemed soul requires a restored body which requires a renewed environment. The Bible, which begins with a righteous, unfallen man in a perfect setting, ends with glorified man in Paradise.

Only through the redemptive recreative work of Jesus Christ can man enter the Garden from which disobedience excluded him. John Warwick Montgomery writes, "The cherubim still stand at Eden's gate with 'a flaming sword which turns every way, to keep the way of the tree of life" (Gen. 3:24). All of us . . . are caught, as Steinbeck well puts it, 'east of Eden.' The only way back (John 14:6) is a route that passes by a Cross set high on a hill, outside a city wall. Only by the sword of the Spirit (Eph. 6:17), which is the Word of God—Christ Himself—can we overcome the obstacle that keeps us from Paradise, for that obstacle is the result of our own sin and self-centeredness, and only Christ Himself can remove it by His atoning death" (*Principalities and Powers*, Bethany Fellowship, 1973, p. 57). The Good News of the Bible which binds together the gardens of Genesis 2 and

Revelation 22 is that God's love and grace make it possible for lost man to "go home again."

A world-famous violinist would never let a redcap or a baggageman carry his costly Stradivarius, but handled it himself for safety's sake. But one day on a crowded railroad platform he was accidently pushed into the path of a heavily laden baggage truck. His precious violin lay smashed into dozens of pieces, seemingly beyond all repair. Blinded by tears, the celebrated violinist dropped to his knees to gather up the dozens of pieces, even the tiniest of fragments. He took them to the shop of an old violin maker who after scrutiny said it would take two years for him to mend the instrument. Two years later the violinist received his violin as good as new. A perfect violin had been painstakingly recreated out of those broken fragments.

God has purposed to restore and glorify every believer. He is out to refashion him like Christ. He will not settle for anything less. Nor will He fail. It is at the Second Coming that we shall be made like Christ and His plan completed. In the meantime, God desires transformation to be progressively taking place. Top priority for every genuine believer is to consistentl‌y strive to grow more like Him.

Let's not thwart the Master Artist as He seeks to rub off the rough edges, straighten out the crooked lines, smooth out the bumpy spots, and polish the ragged marble. Let's work out our own salvation with fear and trembling (Phil. 2:12-13), cooperating with the Holy Spirit as He works in us both to will and to do of His good pleasure, changing us from glory to glory. Then some day the Master Artist will present us faultless before the presence of His glory with exceeding joy, perfectly resembling the Fairest Lord Jesus.

Then the Psalmist's statement will be fully realized, "What is man . . . For thou hast made him a little lower than the angels, and has crowned him with glory and honour" (8:4-5).

Till then, may our prayer be, "Let the beauty of Jesus be seen in me."